Classic Food and Restaurants

OF THE

UPPER PENINSULA

RUSSELL M. MAGNAGHI

AMERICAN PALATE

Published by American Palate
A Division of The History Press
Charleston, SC
www.historypress.com

Cover image: *Superior View*.

First published 2022

Manufactured in the United States

ISBN 9781467149549

Library of Congress Control Number: 2022931438

Contents

Acknowledgements

John Ageropoulos, Marquette, Michigan
Judy Anderson, Mequon, Wisconsin
Patricia T. Appleberry, Marquette, Michigan
Robert R. Archibald, Gwinn, Michigan
Christy Batz, Lake Linden, Michigan
Ted Bays, Marquette, Michigan
Ted Bogdan, Marquette, Michigan
Hans Burtscher, Grand Hotel, Mackinac Island, Michigan
Central Upper Peninsula and University Archives, Northern Michigan
University, Marquette, Michigan
James Christie, Escanaba, Michigan
Lara Clisch, Ishpeming, Michigan
Joe Constance, Marquette, Michigan
Bimbo Constantini, Iron Mountain, Michigan
Mary Crampton, Laurium, Michigan
Don Curto, Marquette, Michigan
Delta County Historical Society, Escanaba, Michigan
Jack Deo, Marquette, Michigan
Bruno Gervasi, Ishpeming, Michigan
Catherine Gervasi, Ishpeming, Michigan
Beth Gruber, Marquette, Michigan
Brian S. Jaeschke, Mackinac Island State Park
John and June Jamrich, Jacksonville, Florida

Catherine Barbiere Johnson, Marquette, Michigan
James Johnson, Marquette, Michigan
Diane D. Kordich, Marquette, Michigan
Phyllis Serappi La Branche, Escanaba, Michigan
James and Natalie La Freniere, North Lake, Michigan
Charles and Karen Lindquist, Escanaba, Michigan
William G. Lockwood, East Lansing, Michigan
Yvonne Hiipäkkä Lockwood, East Lansing, Michigan
Paul Lucas, Marquette, Michigan
Marquette Regional History Center, Marquette, Michigan
Michigan Technological University Archives, Houghton, Michigan
Nathan D. Mileski, Marquette, Michigan
Jane L. Milkie, Marquette, Michigan
Russell Olds, Nashville, Tennessee
Sonia Ott, Wetmore, Michigan
Mary Padakis, Marquette, Michigan
Lore Ann Parent, Marquette, Michigan
Doris Pelonnpää, Ishpeming, Michigan
Donna Peterson, Marquette, Michigan
Peter White Public Library, Marquette, Michigan
Ernest Pretto, Crystal Falls, Michigan
Dante Pricco, Bessemer, Michigan
Martin Reinhardt, Gichi-namebini-Ziibing/Marquette, Michigan
Millie Roberts, Marquette, Michigan
Don Ryan, Marquette, Michigan
Boli Soderberg, Marquette, Michigan
State Library of Michigan, Lansing, Michigan
Frederick Stonehouse, Marquette, Michigan
Michael and Sonia Stucko, Marquette, Michigan
Paul A. Sturgul, Hurley, Wisconsin
Superior View, Marquette, Michigan
Robert Tagatz, Grand Hotel, Mackinac Island, Michigan
Cody Teneyck, Sault Ste. Marie, Michigan
Edward G. Voss, Ann Arbor, Michigan
Jason White, Mackinac Island, Michigan
Laura Gallizioli Young, Sun City, Arizona

Preface

My personal interest in Upper Peninsula food goes back to growing up in restaurant-rich San Francisco, California, working in my dad's Swiss Italian Sausage Factory and enjoying summers amid orchards in the Santa Clara (now Silicon) Valley. When I arrived in Marquette in the fall of 1969, one of the first questions I asked was, "Where is the best Finnish restaurant in Marquette?" My Finnish American informant responded, "Finnish restaurants do not exist here because Finns only eat fish and white food." My quest for the food heritage of the region began at that moment, since everyone has a food-related story to tell. Over the years, I have been aided by countless people across the region who have provided me with answers as to the foodways of their ancestors. There were visits to Pricco's bakery in Bessemer or the Wine Press Bar in Iron Mountain and its weekly porketta roast. I was told that the original pasty was so large it had to be eaten holding it in two hands. Stories of pasty shops and candy stores and soda fountains were everywhere when sought. Hans Burtscher, former executive chef at the Grand Hotel, and other folks provided me with recipes. A fascinating story grew and developed since much of food history is based on recollections and discussions of the tastes and aromas of food.

Then I turned to libraries and archives throughout the Upper Peninsula and Lower Michigan, whose staffs readily shared their expertise and materials. One individual who helped push this study along was a foodie and good friend, Gene Whitehouse, who, when he heard what I was undertaking, said, "What food story of the UP? It doesn't have one." All of these individuals have aided my quest and allowed me to produce this study dealing with classic food, beverages and restaurants of the region. So, yes, Gene, here is the story that you thought did not exist.

Introduction

The Upper Peninsula of Michigan is a unique and little-understood region of the United States. It is separated from the Lower Peninsula of Michigan by the Straits of Mackinac and is considered part of the Midwest, but it is seen by many as part of Canada or Wisconsin. It is a forested environment washed by Lakes Michigan, Huron and Superior on three sides and attached to northern Wisconsin on the fourth. Of Michigan's population of 10 million, the UP is home to over 300,000 people. Throughout the centuries, food has had a major social, cultural and religious impact on the people.

This is a journey into the food world of this exceptional land for those who live here and for visitors. Given its forested and rural environment, the UP clings to foods utilized by Native Americans. Immigrants to the region from many countries, including the French and English, all accepted the traditional foods and brought with them new foods.

The local Anishinaabe (Ojibwa and Odawa), who were unable to farm due to the climate, lived off the land fishing, hunting and gathering. When the French arrived in the seventeenth century, they introduced apples, pears and peas, which they shared with the Native people, and in turn, they were introduced to the local diet. This was the beginning of foodways that were a creolization of two cultures. The British who came later were a bit restrained but followed the same course. They introduced the potato. By the mid-nineteenth century, the fur trade was replaced by the development of the copper, iron, fishing and timber industries. These industries did not attract American-born laborers, and the UP was open to immigrants who arrived by the thousands.

Of the myriad nationalities that arrived—French Canadians, Cornishmen, Germans, Italians, Poles, Croatians, Slovenians, Hungarians, Greeks and Lebanese—the dominant group was the Scandinavians and the Finns. Many of these people found the Upper Peninsula similar to their homeland but with an abundance of local foods—fish, game, berries and potatoes— that they were familiar with and had been the diet of Native Americans. With these immigrants arrived two of the three classic foods of the region— the pasty and the cudighi—while Americans introduced fudge. These new arrivals also brought with them beverages: beer, wine and spirits. Over the years, new immigrants—Asians and Mexicans—have brought their foods as well. There is a continual movement to introduce and embrace new foods, styles of preparation and restaurants. The people collectively known as Yoopers have created a rich world of food in the North Country.

CHAPTER 1

The Early Years to the 1840s

Centuries before the Europeans arrived, every summer the Native people camped at Pe-Quod-e-nonge, "the headland," referring to the northernmost point of Michigan's Lower Peninsula. Here in their birchbark canoes they fished for whitefish, trout, sturgeon, burbot and perch, which were smoked and frozen at the onset of winter and composed 75 percent of their diet. They also gathered a great variety of wild vegetables, berries, fruits, nuts, wild rice and maple sugar.

Native Americans with their own diets first encountered the French—Jesuit missionaries, fur traders and soldiers—in the seventeenth century. The main settlement was Fort Michilimackinac at the northern tip of the Lower Peninsula at the Straits of Mackinac. These early arrivals were unsophisticated in their approach to food. The fur traders were content with pots of soup consisting of peas or wild rice boiled with bacon or lard and possibly seasoned with maple sugar. The Jesuits were not excited about Native food lacking salt and herbs, but provisions were shipped in. The soldiers had government issue: pork and beef, bread and biscuits, corn, peas, grease or lard, flour, wine, brandy and cider. Some of the condiments included olive oil, almonds, dried fruit, cinnamon, pepper, sugar in a variety of forms, onions, mushrooms, salted herbs, capers and anchovies. Everything traveled hundreds and thousands of miles to reach the post from France and Québec.

The Jesuits Jacques Marquette and Louis Nicolas established St. Mary mission at Sault Ste. Marie in 1668 and introduced European agriculture.

They sought to make the Ojibwa/Anishinaabe self-sufficient farmers and introduced peas, pears and apples. Wheat and grapes used in religious services were quickly abandoned, as they could not survive the harsh northern climate. Thus began the creolization of the Upper Peninsula diet.

Marquette and other missionaries also introduced the world to native foods—wild rice, maple sugar, wild berries and fruits—through their reports. Others like Pierre Charlevoix, SJ, who visited the region in 1721, went into detail about the abundance of whitefish, lake trout and other varieties of fish at the Straits. Lacking basic agriculture, there were times of famine in the north woods, and the Native Americans and French turned to "survival foods." Louis André, SJ, wrote about surviving on the inner bark of fir trees and living on a viscous soup based on *tripe de roche* or rock tripe (genus *Umbilicaria*), an edible species of lichen. Another Jesuit and associated Native people survived for two months on a blueberry diet, and others did the same with maple sugar.

The first voyageurs to travel west from Montréal to Mackinac were called *mangeurs de lard* ("pork eaters"), as they traveled on a diet of hard bread and pea soup made with a piece of pork, which was common among French Canadians. Once they were in Indian country, they ate corn or wild rice soup, to which jerky was added, and other food that was conveniently procured.

The French residents at Michilimackinac sat down for a meal consisting of a variety of foods. They first relied on provisions shipped from Montréal and Québec, including dried biscuits, peas, salt pork, bacon, flour, cider, red wine and brandy. Once settled, the French planted vegetable gardens growing herbs and garlic and raised domestic animals such as sheep, pigs and poultry. They modified their diet to fit local conditions. They also hunted wild game, adding deer, bear, rabbit, grouse, beaver, squirrel and porcupine to their diet. Fish—whitefish, trout and sturgeon—was readily available in the Straits and traded from Native people or fished by the French.

In 1749, Michel Chartier Lotbinière noted that Native people "prefer living on corn, fish, and deer or moose grease rather than take the least pain to better their life....The fish they most commonly eat is Whitefish which measures ordinarily twelve to fifteen inches from head to tail....They catch their fish during the month of October at La Grosse Isle [Mackinac Island] where they lay their nets, and after their winter supply of fish is caught they smoke it or put it [in] the snow to preserve it." Fish and meat were sometimes mixed with ground corn to create the dish *sagamaté*. The

French dwellings and gardens at Fort Michilimackinac, circa 1750. *Author.*

All cooking at this time was done in the hearth. *Mackinac State Park.*

The French introduced outdoor ovens, where bread was baked and coffee roasted. *Author.*

Anishinaabe and the French settlers added migratory birds—ducks, geese and passenger pigeons—to their diet using flintlock muskets and lead shot. Corn, wild rice, berries and maple sugar were incorporated into the French Canadian cuisine. The French steeped dried corn in wood ash lye to take off the rind and produce hominy, making it more digestible. At this time, dome-shaped outdoor ovens appeared as the French introduced commercial baking of wheat bread to the region.

The British took over French Canada and occupied Fort Michilimackinac beginning in 1760 and remained until 1796. Both the British and the French were surrounded by wild chokecherries, pin cherries, sand cherries, mountain ash and wild plums, which were easily gathered and either eaten as picked or dried for winter use. John Askin, a trader and farmer, developed a large farm that provided access to a greater variety of grains and vegetables, which included buckwheat, oats, rye, peas, potatoes, cabbage, turnips and spinach. Now there was a greater reliance on domesticated animals, which provided a more varied and interesting diet than the heavily fish-based meals of the French.

Women prepared both wild and domestic meats. *Mackinac State Park.*

The daily ration of a soldier in the Eighth Regiment at Michilimackinac was one pound of bread, half a pound of pork, one ounce of butter, one-quarter pint of peas and one ounce of oatmeal. Rations were issued weekly and pooled by a group of men known as a "mess." Each room of the barracks housed two messes. Since Michilimackinac was at the end of the supply line, at times the rations arrived spoiled or were of poor quality. Frequently, men supplemented them with fish and local produce. Finally, meals were topped off with coffee, tea, brandy, rum, spruce beer or wine when available, but there was always water.

Across the Lake Superior country, traders and pioneers continued to live off the land. For instance, in 1798, English traders in the region were kept alive during the winter on a diet of wild rice and maple sugar. At other times, dried bison meat obtained through trade, beaver tails and swamp cranberries along with ducks were added to their diet.

The American explorers who penetrated the region beginning in 1820 provide written insights to the early cuisine of the region in their journals and reports. The basic provisions of these expeditions consisted of corn,

A typical mess created by French and British soldiers at Fort Michilimackinac. *Author.*

Over the years, lunch in the woods had little changed. *Superior View.*

Native Americans baking bread in a frying pan. *Superior View*.

flour, bacon, crackers, beef tongue, cheese and dried venison. Pork fat and beans were eaten at breakfast and supper. At Fort Mackinac on Mackinac Island, Lewis Cass enjoyed a table with a variety of fine food. Passenger pigeons were readily available. Thomas McKenney passed through the region in 1826 and considered a meal of fish downed with tea a "feast." At Sault Ste. Marie, an Irish immigrant, John Johnston, and his family provided McKenney with a fine meal in the wilderness. McKenney was impressed with "the variety, the cooking, and the exquisite preparation of the beaver's tail," and he was served fine wines at the edge of civilization. After his meal, he concluded that the meal prepared by the Johnston women was "in a style that would vie with the skill of the professed cooks of Washington."

In the summer of 1848, Louis Agassiz led a canoe party up the St. Mary's River toward Sault Ste. Marie, and his journal provides interesting insights into wilderness dining. The canoe was "distinguished by a frying-pan rising erect over the prow as a figure-head, an importance very justly conferred on the culinary art in this wilderness, where nature provides nothing that can be eaten raw except blueberries." At one point, Agassiz and others ventured into the wilds and shot some passenger pigeons, which were roasted on a spit in the ground. He also pointed out that while traveling in the wilderness, if you ran out of supplies, the land would supply a snared rabbit or two, and you could always rely on rock tripe.

The party was supplied with food common to wilderness travel: salt pork, ham, potatoes, peas, beans, flour, hard bread, rice, sugar, butter, coffee, tea, pickles and condiments. When they landed for the evening, the voyageurs prepared for dinner. One kneaded the dough, while others fried or roasted the fish or cooked pork or ham. Pork dumplings were preferred by the men, who also occasionally made rice pudding. Everything was prepared in a large camp kettle suspended over the fire. Finally, Agassiz was fascinated by how the voyageurs made bread with flour, water and salt kneaded well and baked in a frying pan that "turned out excellent bread, perfectly light and well-tasted." He concluded that on such a trip in the wilderness, "one's taste becomes unsophisticated in the woods." Maple sugar was always readily available. The men drank coffee, while the canoeists favored tea, considering it refreshing after a day of hard paddling.

CHAPTER 2

Settlement and Food

The days of the voyageur and the explorer were fading by the decade of the 1840s as the fur trade ended and life changed at Sault Ste. Marie and Mackinac Island. In the interior of the Lake Superior country in 1844–45, copper and iron were discovered and mines and mills developed. As a result of this nascent industrialization, Sault Ste. Marie became the gateway town into the Lake Superior region. The cool summer weather and fishing in the St. Mary's River attracted tourists and transients to the mines, and by 1846, hotels and saloons were established. These hotels offered the first dining experiences in the region. At the Soo, the Van Anden House advertised that "no pain will be spared for the comfort and accommodation of visitors," and soon the table was overflowing with snipes shot by guests. The Bowling Saloon with attached eating house could be compared "with any establishment of the kind in the state, whose meals, together with a cup of good coffee and other refreshments, can be had at all hours for a reasonable price." A year later, the Ste. Marie Hotel was "unsurpassed of any hotel north of Detroit."

This concern for the well-being of the traveler found its way westward. In the distant Copper Country across Lake Superior in 1847 at the Eagle Harbor House on the Keweenaw Peninsula, Hiram Joy rendered the stay of guests agreeable as best he could. The same attitude prevailed in Marquette at the entry to the Iron Country. In 1856, the proprietor of a hotel in Marquette announced that "all the luxuries of the table would be available." At the Soo, shops and saloons were stocked with choicest brands of domestic and imported wines, champagnes, whiskey, rum and brandy. It was becoming easier to find fine food and drink even in the wilds of the Upper Peninsula frontier.

On Mackinac Island, the change from a fur trade economy to that based on tourism was obvious. In the fall of 1824, Samuel C. Lasley opened a large house as a tavern and took in boarders "where every accommodation that the place will afford may be had." In the resort setting, you had the beginnings of fine dining in the region as people went to the island for stays of weeks or months and were seeking comfort food and drink as they enjoyed the cool temperatures and beauty of the region. Their visit to the island was to be an experience to be remembered and one that continues.

With this influx of settlers and tourists, the local cuisine in the late 1840s was based on imported food—beef, pork, hams, dry beef, tongues, flour, cheese, butter, crackers, hard bread, beans, peas, dried fruit, sugar, molasses, coffee, tea "and all necessary cook utensils for the camp." However, incoming settlers, many of whom were farmers, saw the demand for fresh vegetables and potatoes to feed the growing population. As settlers entered the Copper

Family farms allowed miners to work underground and families to main the gardens. *Superior View*.

Country, they found land "where the potato and all vegetables of rapid growth may be raised of a better character and more luxuriant growth than in almost any other section of the country." Farming in this new era got started in the summer of 1847. A similar development took place in the eastern Upper Peninsula, where dozens of farmers were at work in 1849 providing fresh vegetables and making a handsome profit. Livestock in the form of cattle, sheep and hogs were introduced, and the region began to enter an era of self-sufficiency.

If distant from these farms and their produce, the new arrivals had to rely on the traditional Native American diet of potatoes and whitefish. Considered a delicacy today, this was not the case at that time. One woman in the Copper Country recounted that she had prepared whitefish in every imaginable form—fried, broiled, boiled, roasted, smoked, barbecued, poached—and she had run out of ideas and then noted it was only October, with nearly six months of winter approaching. Since many of the early Americans came from New England, their two most characteristic foods— donuts and mincemeat pie—were introduced. Native Americans varied the diet by peddling maple sugar, blueberries and other wild berries. So in reality, when all of the food sources are compiled and analyzed, conditions were not as bad as they seemed on first observation.

CREOLIZATION OF FOOD CONTINUES

Wild Rice

Several foods—wild rice, maple sugar, mushrooms, berries—native to the Upper Peninsula and used by Native Americans were introduced to the Euro-Anglo diet for the continuation of the creolization of foodways. Wild rice was the nutritious grain of Native Americans, since corn was next to impossible to cultivate given the northern latitude. The Menominee, located in the southern UP, were known as the "wild rice people." In 1673, Jacques Marquette, SJ, described in detail their large rice fields and their method of gathering and preserving wild rice. Wild rice was readily used by French fur traders and explorers who obtained it from the Indians and varied their diet of dried peas and corn. However, given the difficulty in cultivating it due to fluctuating water levels, it never became a farm crop for Americans. Furthermore, the arrival of Americans brought with it the timber industry that caused soil erosion and destruction of rice beds. The white people had their flour and grains and little interest in wild rice. It was not until the late twentieth century that Native Americans in the UP began the reintroduction of wild rice.

Maple Sugar and Syrup

Maple syrup production is the oldest agricultural enterprise in North America and the Upper Peninsula. It takes forty to fifty gallons of sap, depending on the sugar content, to produce a gallon of syrup, and more for sugar. The first accounts of the use of maple sugar come to us from the Jesuit missionaries. They left us with invaluable accounts of the maple tree, "maple water" or sap processing and its uses among the Native Americans and the Jesuits. These accounts were common throughout the northern reaches of their missions. Sebastian Rale, SJ, noted in October 1722 that he disliked Indian cooked meat and smoked fish and his "simple and light food" was boiled corn, "a kind of hominy," that was flavored with maple sugar. He continued his narrative, describing the process of making maple sugar, and to better explain maple sugar, he compared the liquor brought from the tree to the liquor found in Caribbean Island sugar cane.

Alexander Henry, an English trader living with the Indians, provided insights into the Indian diet and the amount of maple sap needed to make sugar and syrup during the early spring—maple sugar time—when natural food was scarce. On April 25, 1763, the labor at the sugar bush ended, and Henry and seven male and female Ojibwa returned to the trading post with 1,900 pounds of sugar along with 36 gallons of syrup. During their stay at the sugar bush, they consumed 300 pounds of maple sugar, which, despite what they hunted and fished for, was the main food source for the previous month. Scholars have estimated that 2 pounds of sugar per day is sufficient food for one adult, and thus they had enough food to sustain them for 118 days. It takes about 50 gallons of sap to make 1 gallon of syrup. The 36 gallons of syrup mentioned by Henry represents 1,800 gallons of sap. Since it also takes about 50 gallons of sap to make 8 pounds of sugar, the 1,900 pounds of sugar represent some 11,875 gallons of sap. To add the amount of sugar the group consumed, they must have collected about 13,675 gallons of maple sap that spring.

Traditionally, maple sugar was an important part of the Native diet, and in 1828, the Native Americans on Mackinac Island produced 5,000

Native American family at their sugar bush in Hannahville, Michigan. *Superior View.*

pounds of maple sugar. Twenty years later, a report came out that the Native Americans in Chippewa County made 325,000 pounds, or over 147 tons, of maple sugar, worth $22,750 ($749,394 today). They were operating at industrial capacity.

Two areas in the eastern Upper Peninsula were well known for their maple trees. Sugar Island was so named since it was covered with maple trees. Its finished product was sold in Sault Ste. Marie. Two hundred trees would yield sap enough to make 100 pounds of sugar in a good week's run. In the early nineteenth century, during the maple season, the populace on Mackinac Island would leave for several weeks. They established camps in the woods on neighboring Bois Blanc Island and processed maple sap. It turned into a major social event for the islanders and broke up their winter solitude. As early settlers arrived in the UP, they entered the woods in March and April, collected sap and boiled it into syrup and sugar. In 1859, they produced 9,408 pounds of maple sugar along with 244 gallons of syrup.

The Native Americans traditionally placed sugar in birchbark containers called mococks containing a quarter of a pound to one hundred pounds. They peddled mococks of maple sugar from door to door through UP towns. Smaller mococks were artistically decorated with colored porcupine quills. These were purchased by summer tourists as souvenirs for their artistic designs rather than the sugar within.

Maple sugar and syrup was and is popular with Yoopers to the present day. It is used as syrup for pancakes, but it has also been used to make candy and ice cream. During the season, folks would go to a sugar bush and enjoy "maple taffy"—thick syrup on snow—and healthier maple sugar replaced sugar candy for children. Newspapers discussed sugar making and were filled with recipes for maple pralines, parfaits, Charlotte Russe, pudding, maple-tapioca jelly and maple seafoam. By the 1930s, maple sugar socials were popular as fundraising events among church groups. During World Wars I and II, when sugar was rationed, farmers in the Upper Peninsula were encouraged to produce maple sugar.

Over the years, maple syrup was primarily a cottage industry and provided supplemental income to farmers. However, Reverend William Poyseor, an Episcopal priest at Crystal Falls, developed a dairy farm and a sugar bush. By 1906, his commercial plant was processing maple syrup—seven hundred to eight hundred gallons annually—sold locally and shipped to twelve states. His enterprise became one of the largest maple processing plants in Michigan. Another successful sugar camp was located on Grand Island and operated by the Cleveland Cliffs Iron Company in the 1930s. It refined hundreds of gallons of syrup that were sold locally and shipped out of state. The company also kept a supply for sales to summer tourists who visited the island.

Despite these success stories, in the 1920s and 1930s, when attempts were made to develop a commercial industry in the UP, nothing materialized. In 2021, the Michigan Maple Sugar Association listed seven maple sugarhouse locations in the Upper Peninsula, and their products are available in UP groceries alongside national brands. A number of maple sugar shops produce candies as well as syrups. The most prominent is Besteman Maple Products in Rudyard, whose products include maple syrup, candy, granulated sugar, maple creams, cotton candy and maple glazed nuts.

Berries

Given its northern location, the Upper Peninsula has been home to a variety of berries that were one of the traditional foods of the Native Americans and were readily introduced into European diets. The French and English at Fort

Strawberries and especially blueberries were sold by Native Americans.
Superior View.

Michilimackinac had access to American mountain ash, Arctic brambles, barberries, blackberries, huckleberries, mulberries, raspberries and service or June berries. As settlers entered the UP, they gathered and dried the berries or made jam with them.

By 1857, local newspapers promoted the fact that there were a variety of hardy fruits—cranberry, blueberry, raspberry, whortleberry, strawberry— that were available for picking. The wild raspberries had "the finest flavor," while the indigenous strawberry was "remarkable and abundant." Currants were rare but were growing to "considerable perfection," while gooseberries were available as well. The newcomers did not have to go far to find berries, as they were literally surrounded by them. If you did not want to pick your own, you could purchase them from Native Americans who sold berries, especially blueberries, from door to door. Later in the nineteenth century, when the Finns, Swedes and Norwegians arrived, they found that they had arrived in a berry paradise similar to what they had in their homelands, and berry picking was a time to visit and socialize.

Cranberries

Cranberries were found across the Upper Peninsula from Ontonagon to Sault Ste. Marie. The cranberries concentrated along the St. Mary's River were considered "much larger and finer" than berries found on the East Coast. During the October harvest season, half of the Indian families would be absent from their villages gathering these berries in the swamps. By 1855, all of the French and English Canadian and American settlers along the river gathered and preserved large quantities of these berries. They even became an important export commodity to Québec and the eastern states. One of the local settlers boasted that he exported several tons annually. Although difficult to find today, wild cranberries are gathered by those who seek them.

The only cranberry farm in Michigan is the Centennial Cranberry Farm located in Paradise at the Whitefish Point. John Clarke, realizing that wild cranberries grew in the area, developed a farm of domesticated cranberries in 1876, thus the farm's name. He first hired Native Americans as pickers, and they set up camps and socialized, tying in the two cultures. The farm continues in operation, and the cranberries are seen as "red gold," as in a given year, truckloads totaling eighty tons of berries have been taken from the farm. The farm gift shop sells cranberry sauce, cranberry butter and fresh berries in the fall.

Strawberries

Both wild and tame strawberries were available. In 1893, it was announced that Chippewa County "beats the world for wild strawberries." There were so many "small but very sweet" strawberries and raspberries on Lime Island in the St. Mary's River that it was difficult to walk on the island without crushing them. Tame strawberries were either grown in gardens or were shipped by the train load and supplied the population. At county fairs, the best wild and tame canned strawberries, preserves and jams were awarded prizes. Tasty but tiny wild strawberries are available to those who seek them, but it is a time-consuming project to gather them.

Blueberries

White people replaced Indians gathering blueberries across the Upper Peninsula. The Depression of 1873 really caused people to turn to the land for subsistence, and then a cottage industry developed that continued for nearly a century. By 1894, 6,500 cases or 3,250 bushels of "northern wild blueberries" were shipped to Chicago, St. Paul, Minneapolis and south to Memphis. Three years later, the blueberry crop in the vicinity of Marquette was worth between $60,000 and $70,000.

A woman ready to enter the blueberry fields in the 1930s. *Superior View.*

At first, "blueberry trains" brought folks to their favorite picking locations, and later Model Ts took families into blueberry fields, where they established tent camps and picked for nearly a month. During the Great Depression of the 1930s, people made money and survived by picking berries. In the twenty-first century, blueberry picking remains an important social activity for many in the UP, but the export of berries has come to an end.

Thimbleberry

If the blueberry is plentiful and can be shipped, the thimbleberry is a special berry. Thimbleberry plants (*Rubus parviflorus*) are native to western North America and then, separated by about six hundred miles, are found in the Great Lakes region. Newly arrived settlers found bright red fruit similar to raspberries growing along roadsides, railroad tracks and in forest clearings in mid- to late summer. However, the berries do not ship well and are not cultivated commercially. A special summer treat, they are eaten raw, dried or made into jam, which is considered a delicacy and sought after by locals and visitors.

JAM PRODUCTION

Upper Peninsula wild berry jams and preserves continue to be a link between the modern world and that of Native Americans and are an iconic food of the UP. The first jam maker was Philetus Church, who settled on Sugar Island downriver from Sault Ste. Marie in the 1850s and found the island covered with wild raspberry bushes. Encouraged by visitors, he developed a jam trade among his other entrepreneurial enterprises. In 1852, he shipped five thousand pounds of jam to Chicago and other cities and sold to passing ship passengers and the local Soo population, and his production increased. Few commercial jam producers rose to meet a demand, as jams and jelly were made for home use while folks sold homemade preserves from roadside stands. Today, jam making is centered in the Copper Country with UP Foods, the Jam Lady and the Wood 'n Spoon making and selling preserves.

There are three major cottage industries producing thimbleberry and other wild jams for sale on the Keweenaw Peninsula, the heartland of wild berries. Paul Mihelcich is the current owner of the Eagle River jam and jelly company known as the Jam Lady, started by his grandmother. His family emigrated from Croatia in about 1885 and have been making thimbleberry jam for a century and selling it for fifty years. Down the road at Lake Linden, UP Foods produces a variety of jams as well.

The Society of St. John was established by Byzantine Catholic monks in 1983 near Eagle Harbor and sought to develop a means of bringing in revenue. They established their kitchen and store, the Jampot, and

Preserves and baked goods are sold by the monks at their Jampot shop. *Author.*

three years later sold their Poorrock Abbey preserves made from local wild berries. Today, it is a gourmet shop selling preserves, sweets and fruit cakes in the summer and shipping in the winter. The thimbleberry jam is a gourmet classic.

WILD FOODS

The woods of the Upper Peninsula are home to a variety of wild foods. Wild leeks, having a flavor of onions and garlic, are considered a delicacy among chefs and foragers. Fiddlehead ferns are also gathered in the woods and used as green vegetables. Mushrooms and morels have a wider appeal. By the late nineteenth century, newspapers were writing about mushroom-gathering parties going to the woods. Newspapers carried important alerts as to when the season began, usually after the first rains in the spring. Mushrooms are an important part of the Polish culinary diet, and the Polish were first in the woods. There were individuals in the Copper Country growing mushrooms in the first decade of the twentieth century, and others grew them in their cellars for their personal use. A Serbian immigrant, John Cashavenda of Ironwood, left iron mining and became a successful commercial mushroom grower in the 1920s. Newspapers always carried alerts warning people to be familiar with mushrooms and avoid poisonous ones. The morels are considered one of the choice items of the wild garden. In 2018, Amy Bachhuber and Rohn Sorensen established the Superior Mycology Company in Houghton and began the year-round indoor cultivation of mushrooms; they also conduct seasonal foraging. Their mushrooms are sold to individuals, brokers, local farmers' markets and the Keweenaw Coop. Bachhuber has been certified by the State of Michigan as a wild mushroom expert. In Skandia, Tonella Farms, which opened in 2016, grow and sell mushrooms available at the Marquette Farmers Market.

The author John Voelker had an interest in mushrooms and hunting for them. His personal library contained numerous books related to the science and collecting of mushrooms. His good friend Ted Bogdan, of Polish ancestry, was a mushroom expert, having grown up in Illinois on a family mushroom farm. The two of them—sometimes joined by the county extension authority on mushrooms, Ingrid Bartelli, and by Dr. Alexander Smith, an authority on mushrooms from the University of Michigan— would hunt for mushrooms and then retire to camp to enjoy the product of the hunt. The mushroom-hunting season began in the middle or later part of May and started with hunting for black morels, followed by white morels. Peppery-flavored oyster mushrooms were next, followed by early chanterelles and Italian porcini, which brought them to September and the end of the season. During the season, grilled mushrooms were a treat for everyone and a favorite of Voelker's. Bogdan's recipe for grilled mushroom is: "Pull the stems of the mushrooms and grill not too close to the heat. Soften them. There was juice in the mushroom that gathered inside first. Wait until it cools off, drink the juice first, then eat the mushroom. True essence of the flavor is the mushroom." When the CBS reporter Charles Kuralt visited Voelker, he tried the mushrooms and declared them one of the three best foods he had ever eaten.

FISH AND GAME

Wild game and fish were important parts of the Native diet, and they were used by the incoming Europeans and Americans, as seen in the French and English diets at Fort Michilimackinac. This continued with the first Americans who arrived. These readily available food sources were used by the settlers who found imported food costly.

Commercial fishing has been part of the development of the UP since the early days. Native Americans, Métis and Euro-Americans used Mackinac Island, the adjacent coast, Sault Ste. Marie and Escanaba and Menominee as major fishing areas. In the 1830s, fisheries developed for local consumption, but an early industry using Native American fishermen shipped salted fish from the area. With the arrival of settlement, the locals turned to fish rather than expensive imported salted meats. Later, Finns, Scandinavians and others either fished for or purchased this ready-made source of protein.

Today, the Fish Trail can be found along the Lake Michigan shoreline between St. Ignace and Manistique. Naubinway, the northernmost community on the Lake Michigan shoreline in the UP, is the largest commercial fishing port on the Great Lakes in the UP. Although there are numerous stores offering fresh and smoked fish, they are dominated by the retailer and wholesaler King's Fish Market. The Lake Superior shoreline has two major fish markets. Francis Thill began commercially fishing in 1948 in the waters off the Garden Peninsula, moved to Marquette in 1959 and opened his shop two years later. The third generation operates the fish shop, selling a variety of seafood, but is known for its fresh and smoked whitefish and lake trout. In Hancock, there is Peterson's Fish Market, which was opened in 1992 by Patricia and Gilmore Peterson, members of the Red Cliff Band of Superior Chippewa. They are fourth-generation fishers

A Munising fisherman in 1900 with what could be considered "a typical catch." *Superior View.*

Above: Women enjoyed fishing as well as men. *Superior View.*

Opposite, top: Unloading fish at Thill's dock in Marquette. *Superior View.*

Opposite, bottom: Smelting in Marquette and other areas of the UP continued into the early 1980s. *Superior View.*

and sell wholesale across the United States. Thus, the ancient practice of fishing remains alive and well in the UP, although highly regulated by state law.

Whitefish's reputation has experienced an ongoing creolization, as it is now served in restaurants across the Upper Peninsula and enjoyed by Yoopers and visitors alike. The outstanding food emporium for whitefish is the Vierling Restaurant in Marquette, serving whitefish in a variety of types: grilled, bites, Cajun style, piccata, tapenade, scampi style and in chowder. Iron Bay Restaurant, located around the corner on the shore of Lake Superior, serves whitefish tater tots, chowder, tacos and whitefish and chips and whimsically advertises, "Our whitefish were in school yesterday" or "Our whitefish traveled over one hundred yards to get here." Most recently, Joe Constance has added a mobile unit serving whitefish in town.

The abundance of birds and ducks with few hunting restrictions allowed groups to have a full larder. *Superior View.*

The consumption of game has also been absorbed by the people who followed the Indians, and it has become an important part of the diet for some people. Hunting for game also provided a social component. The earliest Europeans enjoyed venison, passenger pigeon, duck and beaver, which were readily available.

Settlers who arrived after the region opened continued this culinary tradition. This is seen in the following elaborate feast put on by the St. Andrew Society of Ontonagon on November 30, 1855. St. Andrew is the patron of Scotland, and they were celebrating his feast day. The banquet was held for two hundred people and was presented on "a table groaning under the load of characteristic national dishes, together with all the luxuries which our part of the country affords, and the best wines without limit." The following menu is a composite of native foods of the UP and Scotch cuisine and illustrates how a people used food to celebrate a national event. It also shows how these settlers in far western UP had their diets creolized:

St. Andrew's Festival
Bigelow House
November 30, 1855

SOUPS
Oyster   Vermicelli
GAME
Beavers Tail. Saddle of Caribou. Cranberry Sauce.
Bear Steak. Mountain Ash Sauce.
Porcupine, al La Ontonagon. Buffalo Tongue.
Buffalo Rump roasted. Red Deer. Mashlum Scone.
SCOTCH HAGGIS
Oat Meal Bannocks. Scotch Kail. Beef and Greens
FISH
Mackinac Trout Baked. Mackinac Trout Boiled.
White Fish Baked. Isle Royale Siskowit Boiled.
MEATS
Turkey and Oyster Sauce. Turkey and Celery Sauce.
Mutton and Caper Sauce. Chicken and Mint Sauce.
Ham. Tongue. Round of Beef.
SIDE DISHES
Fillet of Fowl, Celery Sauce. Beef Kidney Stewed in Champagne.
Chicken Pie. Oyster Pie. Tender Loin of Beef Larded.
Veal Pie. Peas Meal Brose.
ROASTS
Turkey Cranberry Sauce. Sirloin of Beef, Chicken. Fillet of Pork.
Leg of Pork. Saddle of Mutton. Alamode Beef.
RELISHES
Pickled Cabbage. Onions. Cucumbers, Beets, Tripe.
VEGETABLES
Green Corn, Green Peas, Green Beans, Tomatoes. Asparagus.
PASTRY AND CONFECTIONERY
Calves Foot Jelly. Cream Custard. Raspberry Jam Tarts.
Cranberry Jelly Tarts. Pound Cake. Sponge Cake, Wine Jelly.
Blanc Mange. Ice Cream. Jelly Cake. Fruit Cake. Mince Pie. Peach Pie.
Apple Pie, Custard Pie. Floating Island, Gold Cake, Charlotte Russe
FRUIT
Apples. Almonds, Raisins, Figs, Filberts

As the century progressed, deer were openly hunted, although the State of Michigan began to control the hunt by the end of the nineteenth century. Before widespread market hunting ended around 1901, when sale of venison was restricted, sides of deer would appear within hours of the opening of the season in front of meat markets and butcher shops. This became a profitable business for many and depleted the deer population.

Game continued to be part of the diet of people lucky enough to hunt or have friends with extra venison to give away. Service clubs like the Elks, Veterans of Foreign Wars and fraternal organizations like the Knights and Ladies of Kaleva invited folks to attend a venison feed as a fundraiser and social event. Some of these organizations included in a feed not only venison but also beaver, squirrel and a variety of geese and ducks. Individuals had home venison dinners for friends; schools served venison stew as part of their weekly menu for students; in some homes, venison replaced turkey at Thanksgiving at the end of the hunting season.

Today, the firearm hunting season lasts from November 15 to 30. In many areas of the UP, opening day is considered a holiday, with school and businesses suspended for the day. The deer hunt and going to camp have also always been seen as social events adorned with good food and beverage. In the 1950s, one camp included a barrel of fresh oysters, the finest bourbon was served and a hired chef provided excellent meals—all done in the heart of the woods, recorded by a commercial photographer.

How did game wardens and the Department of Natural Resources deal with seized game? Venison was served at the Marquette Branch Prison as a Christmas treat, and less fortunate people were given venison through the Salvation Army.

During hunting season, newspapers carried recipes and directions to make sure that the hunter processed the deer correctly to avoid the gamey taste of the meat. A new cottage food industry arose processing deer meat and making deer sausage and salami, and it continues to the present.

Not only are deer hunted, but Canada geese and wild ducks are as well. When Europeans arrived in America, it is estimated that three to five billion passenger pigeons were known to darken the sky as they passed over. In the nineteenth century, hundreds and thousands of passenger pigeons, whose flyway went across the eastern UP, were hunted. Some were eaten locally, but barrels filled with pigeons were also shipped to urban markets. The last passenger pigeon died in 1914 at the Cincinnati Zoo.

Italian immigrants enjoyed eating songbirds, which were taken with special mattress traps and glues placed on tree limbs that caught the birds.

A successful Yooper hunter poses with birds, rabbits and a deer, prepared for a feast. *Superior View.*

Given the small size of songbirds, at least ten birds had to be served per person at a dinner. Children defeathered them, and then they were stewed and served on a bed of polenta. In 1908, a state game warden in Dickinson County was furious with Italian railroad workers who feasted on songbirds and wild game, including squirrels and porcupines. He said next "they would be eating skunk." For these immigrants, the woods continued to be seen as a source of food.

Rabbits were also seen as a popular food, both tender and delectable. Americans and many European immigrants were fond of rabbit and either bought it in butcher shops when it was available or hunted it in the winter months. Native Americans in the Copper Country snared rabbits and sold them to meet this demand. During the Depression of the 1930s, rabbits, pheasants, sharp-tailed grouse and woodcock were readily hunted, and sportsmen's clubs would have rabbit stew banquets for their members. In the 1970s, Northern Michigan University president John X. Jamrich, who was of Slovak heritage, snared rabbits in the center of Marquette. Rabbit hunting continues to be conducted in the Peninsula.

INTRODUCED FOODS: POTATOES, APPLES, RUTABAGA AND CELERY

Beyond the food items of nature, there was the introduction of four notable crops to the UP: potatoes, apples, rutabagas and celery. The potato has been a major part of the food story in the region. The French did not introduce the potato to the UP in the seventeenth century. As informants told Peter Kalm in the 1740s, the common potato was not planted in Canada/New France because "they do not like them and laugh at the English who are so fond of them." Once the English conquest took place in 1760, the potato found a new home in Canada and arrived in the Upper Peninsula. The sandy soil around Fort Michilimackinac was ideal for potato cultivation. John Askin planted them outside the fort, as did others. As happened elsewhere, potatoes provided a local inexpensive food source that did not have to be imported.

Fifty miles to the north at Sault Ste. Marie, Irish immigrant John Johnston, a community leader engaged in the fur trade, farmed as well, and potatoes proved to be a popular item to cultivate. In July 1822, a reporter from the *Detroit Gazette* reached the Soo and wrote, "Potatoes, oats, pease and garden stuffs generally succeed with certainty every year." In 1826, when the commissioner of Indian Affairs, Thomas McKenney, visited Sault Ste. Marie, he was impressed with "the finest quality" potatoes being cultivated and was amazed at agricultural foodstuffs being grown in the barren north country.

The early Protestant and Catholic missionaries arriving in the 1820s reintroduced agriculture to the Native people. This was an attempt to create sedentary life and assimilate them according to nineteenth-century American standards, and potatoes were accepted and became part of the Native diet. With the opening of the copper mines in the 1840s, Ojibwa farmers found a market for their potatoes, which provided an inexpensive and nourishing food source for the miners. With the settlement of the UP, farmers also found a market for their crop of "unequalled potatoes." Potato farming became a major economic activity and was promoted by mining companies as a means of keeping miners well fed, thus sustaining a viable labor force.

The potato went on to become a staple and profitable farm crop in the UP. It was overseen by the Michigan State University experimental farm in Chatham and by the Upper Peninsula Potato Association, which held annual potato congresses to identify the prime variety. Winners eventually went to the state potato congress held in Grand Rapids. The Upper Peninsula Development Agency encouraged locals to buy "Cloverland potatoes," and the Cohodas vegetable and fruit provisioners sold bags of Lake Superior Brand Potatoes.

Potato farming even expanded to growing seed potatoes that were sold around the United States. In the early 1980s, Peter Vitton of Hancock had a contract with McDonald's to grow seed potatoes for its farm clients throughout the country. Today, there are ten large efficient potato growers in the central Upper Peninsula planting thirty-five varieties. Of these farms, the Melvin Johnson Potato Farm in Sagola, operating since the 1930s, produces eleven to eleven and a half million pounds of potatoes each year. It has contracts with Kroger and Costco and sells to local outlets. Thus, this historic UP industry continues to flourish some 260 years after its introduction.

In 1959, August Janke opened Ely's Potato Chip Company in Escanaba. It produced private-label chips for A&P, Supervalu, Red Owl, Piggly Wiggly and Northland grocers and became one of the largest potato chip manufacturers in the United States. Unfortunately, ill health caused Janke to sell the plant in 1969. In the vicinity at Watson, potato farmers Paul and Jeanette Van Damme opened Superior Frozen French Fries in 1971 and served a large market before closing in 1995.

The apple was another crop that found a home in the Upper Peninsula, first introduced by Jesuit missionaries at Sault Ste. Marie and the Straits of Mackinac. They were cultivated by the Native Americans and incoming settlers. Farming families tried to plant at least three or four varieties of

In the nineteenth century, apples were growing across the Upper Peninsula. *Superior View.*

apples so they had apples through the entire harvest, with some varieties storing well into March. As with potatoes, immigrants, especially Swedes, turned to apples for home and commercial consumption. The heyday of apple growing was the 1920s and 1930s, and it has declined due to weather conditions—early frosts—and the lack of markets. However, two apple farmers continue to cultivate some six hundred trees between them and sell apples to local residents.

The third introduced crop—little known to Americans—is the rutabaga (*Braasica napobtassica*). It was an intentional or unintentional crossing of the turnip and the wild cabbage. Being a hardy plant that likes cool weather and hard frosts to sweeten it, the rutabaga found a home in Northern Europe, where Norwegians refer to it as the "orange of the North." It is a healthy food with few calories and filled with vitamins and minerals. The Canadians and English called it swede, and others referred to it as a yellow turnip, Swedish turnip and Canadian turnip. It entered the English language in 1799 as the "rutabaga," derived from the Swedish *rotabagge*, or "baggy root." The vegetable has never been popular with Americans, who are rather mystified by rutabagas in groceries.

The rutabaga had ethnic origins coming into the Upper Peninsula. The Cornish use it in pasties, the Irish include it in colcannon and the Scandinavians and Finns have many uses for it in their cuisines. As a result, when these immigrants arrived in the UP, they were pleased to find that their traditional food could thrive in the environment and they would not have to import it from Ontario. The early Finnish and Swedish farmers planted rutabagas, and they were followed by American farmers who saw there was a profitable market for the crop. As a result, more than any place in the United States, people in the UP readily encountered the rutabaga in groceries, at county fairs, in church and lodge suppers and in hotel dining rooms, where mashed rutabagas were often on the menu. As a result, although not as well known as the pasty, it is part of the Yooper diet in many homes. The humble rutabaga found a home in this corner of the United States.

Another little-known crop grown in the Upper Peninsula was Golden Plume celery, cultivated in muck land in Newberry beginning in 1886. Two farmers grew the crop: John G. Van Tuyl, an immigrant from the Netherlands cultivated the O.K. Celery Farm, and Harry L. Harris operated the Newberry Celery Farm. In flavor, it proved an equal to the more famous Kalamazoo celery, and orders poured in, so that in 1891, 450,000 plants were set out. Four years later, celery farming was seen as a major industry in Luce County, and there was talk that the celery farms would become the

John Van Tuyl in his O.K. Celery Garden, Newberry, Michigan, circa 1915. *Superior View.*

largest in Michigan. Celery was shipped to Detroit, Grand Rapids, Duluth, Chicago, New York City and Toronto. Newberry celery was served in hotel dining rooms in the UP, Chicago and New York City, where it was listed as "Newberry Celery" on the menus and in rail dining cars. Yoopers watched for newspaper announcements about the arrival of Newberry celery in groceries. The local athletic teams were known as the Celery City Cagers and the Celeryites.

For over sixty years, Newberry celery was the pride of the UP, and then decline set in. Blight, demand for Green Pascal celery from California and problems with natural fertilizer caused the farms to close by the early 1950s, but for over sixty years, it was a classic crop in the region.

CHAPTER 3

Iconic Foods of the Upper Peninsula

PASTY, FUDGE, CUDIGHI

THE PASTY

Three iconic foods have developed in the Upper Peninsula. The most famous to the region is the pasty, which hails from Cornwall, a small province in southwestern England—and to be clear, it is pronounced "pass-tee." It is best described as a self-standing pie made with meat, vegetables and seasonings. This story is complex, from its historical development, to its ingredients, to its acceptance by other nationalities. It never caught on as a widespread national dish in the United States, and today, it has a limited range, including Grass Valley, California; Butte, Montana; southwestern Wisconsin; and the Upper Peninsula.

The simple pasty dish has a lengthy history along with an equal amount of lore connected with it going back to Roman times. It was through the Old French word *paste* that the word entered Middle English as *pastee* about 1300. Medieval English bakers felt that food "cooked more satisfactorily" in a crust or coffin, as they referred to it, rather than being stewed over a fire. Its quality of manufacture and ingredients were regulated by city and royal ordinances. The pasty also appears in the literature of the time: Chaucer's *Canterbury Tales* around 1386 mentions pasties, and it appears in three of William Shakespeare's plays with a variety of meanings beginning in the 1580s.

Over the centuries, the ingredients varied with the times. Venison was very popular, but if necessary, goat or "rock venison" was used. Cookbooks described chicken liver and bacon pasties. *Butte's Heritage* cookbook of 1976 described not only Cornish pasties but under "Butte Pasties with Variations" also listed the use of leftover roast, ground round, chicken, elk, venison and even an egg pasty. People living close to the sea might fill their pasty with a variety of fish, while others added lamb or made leek and herb pies. As Upper Peninsula historian Mac Frimodig wrote, "There was even a variation of the pilchard pie called the 'starry-gazy' in which whole sardines were introduced to their final resting place in a vertical position so that their heads protruded through the top crust, enabling them to watch their own last rites." The variety of fillings is so great that there is an old Cornish saying: "The Devil is afraid to come into Cornwall, for fear of being baked in a pasty."

The pasty developed as an important part of the Cornish diet, especially among tin and copper miners, although it is now found throughout the United Kingdom. Poor economic conditions forced over 100,000 Cornish people to leave their homeland and seek a better life in the United States beginning in the nineteenth century. They found jobs in coal mines and worked in the lead mines of southwest Wisconsin. With the discovery of copper and iron deposits in Michigan's Upper Peninsula in the late 1840s, Cornish miners moved north through Wisconsin and brought with them the pasty, along with saffron buns.

The stories of the pasty and its use abound. The Cornish miner could carry his self-contained lunch in his warm dinner pail into the mine. These pasties were huge in order to provide calories for their hard work. Cornish people in the Upper Peninsula are usually referred to as "Cousin Jacks" and "Cousin Jennies." So the story goes that one winter when Jenny Phillips tried to stretch her food budget, she scrimped on the beef and pork for her husband's pasties. His immediate reaction upon returning home was, "Jenny, let's be having a little more mayt in me pasty and not so much turmit and tatey; me stummick's no bloody root cellar, y'know." Then there is the story of a newly married Cousin Jack whose Cousin Jenny (wife) had not yet mastered the art of pasty making. When he returned home from the mine after his first homemade pasty, he complained sorrowfully, "Damme, when I got down the shaft the pasty was all busted up in the pail. Damme, mother made a pasty you could heave down the shaft, and 'it a 'undred feet down, and it wouldn't bust." In 1911, J.H. Harris wrote in *Saints and Sinners*, "When small, a pasty is a snack; when large, it's a meal." A Cornish miner in Bessemer in 1939 talked about how to eat a pasty: "W'at does thee know 'bout pasties? Thee's the kind of a man w'at cut 'n cross the middle and

Iron miner Carlo Pellonpää and his working partner enjoy their pasty lunch. *Superior View.*

let's all that pretty juice run about over the plate. Thee's the kind of man w'at takes 'a right b'out of h'oven gulps it daown."

It was been pointed out that Cornwall is as protective about its pasties as neighboring Devon is about its cream. When the traveling food editors Jane and Michael Stern discussed pasty making in *Real American Food* (1986) with Nancy Lawry in Ishpeming, Michigan, they had to report, "Although Nancy happily told us everything that goes into one of her renowned pasties, she could not provide exact measurements, she said, 'pasties are our reputation, and I'd be worried if someone else got a hold of just how we do it.'"

The Cornish are concerned about what constitutes a "real" Cornish pasty. As a result, there is a community of pasty purists who have constantly regulated the proper pasty preparation and consumption. Bitter controversies have developed over what the exact ingredients should be, how it should be held when eaten and even whether the meat should be diced or sliced or whether hamburger should be used.

The simple pasty can be made using a variety of ingredients and techniques, and here lies the debate as to what constitutes a traditional pasty.

The crust is made with suet/lard/butter, water and flour. The meat can consist of pork and beef, but then a decision has to be made whether it is cubed, diced or ground. Can hamburger or sausage be used? The primary vegetable ingredients, which can be diced or sliced, are rutabagas, onions and potatoes. The inclusion of rutabagas or carrots reopens the controversy, as does the question of how much meat or potatoes should be used. Then, how finely should be the ingredients be cut? Sometimes a small amount of parsley is added for flavor. The recipes change with every cook consulted, and as a result, there is no standard pasty recipe.

Ethnicity has had a further impact on the pasty. The Cornish introduced the pasty, but it is claimed by other nationalities. The first Finns entered the UP in 1864 and made the pasty part of their diet. Thirty years later, a new wave of Finns arrived and were introduced to the pasty by their earlier countrymen. However, the pasty had similar ingredients as their meat pie (*piiräät*), and the Cornish pasty was then believed to be of Finnish origin. The basic rule of thumb is that a Cornish pasty has rutabagas, a Finnish pasty has carrots and a Swedish pasty has onions. One Slavic chef is said

Having finished their pasty lunch, the Werner family enjoys watermelon dessert. *Superior View*.

to have injected a garlicky-flavored sauce into the pasty. Then there are ongoing changes. For some, potatoes have gained a dominant role and rutabagas have given way to finely ground carrots. Diced or chunk meat is sparse in many pasties, and hamburger has even been introduced. The question of gravy is a critical one. In the Upper Peninsula, the use of gravy is considered barbaric by many, while in Butte, Montana, it is traditionally served. Whatever the recipe, many men in the Upper Peninsula will swear that "nobody can bake a pasty like my wife."

The Negaunee mining historian of Cornish heritage, Frank Mathews, had his own way of eating a pasty. He insisted that the pasty should be eaten on its end so that the juices would drain down to the last bite. For him, this was dessert. Then there is the question of what utensils are to be used to eat it. The purists say it must be eaten with the aid of knives and forks, while others claim it can be eaten with the hands.

In the beginning, the pasty was considered a homemade food eaten by miners and at home. Then in the late nineteenth century, the pasty found its way through Methodist Episcopal churches, the church of the Cornish, into the mainstream. It was made and sold by Cornish women as a fundraiser for church groups. For instance, in 1909, the Red Jacket Congregational Church had a well-advertised supper available to the public consisting of a pasty, pickles, coffee, ice cream and cake for thirty-five cents. This quickly spread to other churches, and pasty suppers were served by community groups, as it was an easy meal for women to prepare.

As the twentieth century progressed, the pasty emerged on the market. Time consuming to make, they were first available through bakeries and restaurants with the skilled staff to make them. At first, they were only offered as a specialty item on certain days of the week and then the whole week. However, not every restaurant offered them. In the 1930s, there was talk of a Marquette man with equipment who made one hundred pasties daily, but little was heard of this equipment, and most continued to be handmade.

A further development was making the pasty available through pasty shops. A pioneer of such sales was John Nelson, "the hot pasty man" of Hancock, who waited for trains to briefly stop and provided famished

Pasties are enjoyed by those of all ages. *Superior View*.

The sign that tourists have always sought as they travel through the UP. *Superior View*.

passengers with his pasties, usually regretting that he did not have more of them. By the late 1920s, as tourists began arriving in autos, the pasty shop emerged. In Escanaba in 1929, the Federal Bakery brought pasties to the tourists by supplying meat pasties to La Fleur's Tourist Camp Store and Luncheonette. A market was developing. Among the first to meet the demand in the western UP were Arthur and Alma Massie in Bessemer, who opened their pasty shop on U.S. 2 in 1930 to sell to tourists who were curious about this new food they were encountering. Concerned about a successful market, the Massies faced their shop toward the high school and attracted students as well. Pasties at this time were selling for fifteen cents each. In August 1940, a retired miner, Louis Menghini, and his wife, Lena, opened another early pasty shop in the vicinity on U.S. 2, which became a popular stop for many years. Eating a pasty became part of the vacation experience in the UP.

The pasty easily survived World War II, as its ingredients were not rationed. However, concern grew when Cousin Jennies were encouraged to use day-old roast beef as filling, contrary to grandma's recipe. The pasty was not related to stew, which was "reserved for the Irish." However, it is doubtful that fewer pasties were made during the war.

With the end of the war, a new food era developed in the Upper Peninsula with the success of the pasty shop, especially along the highways now bustling with tourists. One of the first to open on U.S. 2 west of St. Ignace was

Lehto's Pasties in 1947. John Lehto served in World War II, was honorably discharged and had his life before him. Returning home, he opened his pasty shop, which is still owned by the family and serves pasties made with the original recipe to passing travelers.

One of the earliest pasty shops in the Marquette area was Madelyne's Pasties, which operated in the 1950s and then in 1965 moved to Ishpeming. It was the first to fast freeze pasties for shipment. For years, it was one of the largest producers but ceased operation in 1981 when the shop evolved into Lawry's Pasties, eventually with branches in West Ishpeming, Marquette and Harvey. In 1966, Roger Lawry converted forty tons of potatoes, nine tons of vegetables, four tons of lard, twelve tons of flour and fifteen tons of strip steak into enough pasties to stretch five miles from end to end. In the late 1980s, Nancy Lawry told Jane and Michael Stern, authors of *Roadside Food and Good Food*, a guide to regional food, that every morning she started making pasties from scratch and by the end of the day had produced as many as two hundred to four hundred. One Fourth of July, she set a single-day record making seven hundred pasties. The Sterns concluded, "You understand their [pasty] popularity in the cold north woods, when you take possession of a Lawry's pasty. Just to hold this big piece of food imparts a feeling of security."

Today, there are over two dozen pasty shops open across the UP. Online, "The Pasty Guy" provides a list of shops in both the Upper and Lower Peninsulas, rates pasties, lists shippers and allows you to develop your own Pasty Trail through the region. At one time, the Yellow Pages listed a "Pasty" section, probably the only such designation in the country. May 24 is considered national pasty day, and Calumet has an annual Pasty Fest.

Both Michigan Technological University and Northern Michigan University have served pasties for many years on campus on a regular basis and provide their recipes. A Naval recruiter on Tech's campus in the 1990s called the pasty the "Yooper Burrito." The largest pasty ever baked was a monster made by NMU students on October 20, 1978. Baked in an outdoor oven, it included 250 pounds of beef, 400 pounds of potatoes, 75 pounds of carrots and 25 pounds of onions, all wrapped into 250 pounds of dough. It was served to an eager public but was never officially recorded by Guinness World Records.

Word of the pasty has spread beyond the confines of the Upper Peninsula. The *Detroit Free Press* brought the pasty to a larger audience by running stories and advertisements as to where pasties could be ordered. Today, it is common for visitors to take home insulated boxes of frozen pasties or have them shipped to friends and relatives. The pasty has found a home in shops and bakeries in the Lower Peninsula of Michigan from Mackinaw City south to Metro Detroit. Pasty shops can be found in limited numbers around the United States.

The industrial age has reached this crimped-edged food in the UP. In Crystal Falls in 1957, Leroy Nylund began making pasties from scratch and sold them through his grocery. Today, Nylund Pasty has a variety of pasties to select from: beef, beef and rutabaga, beef and pork Cornish pasty, Italian pork, chicken, Mexican and vegetable. The factory supplies pasties to groceries throughout the Upper Peninsula and northern Wisconsin.

On June 24, 2004, California governor Arnold Schwarzenegger was depicted in a newspaper photo holding up a *Lansing State Journal*, wearing a Detroit Pistons jersey and munching on a pasty. This was the Governator's payoff for picking the Los Angeles Lakers in the National Basketball Association finals in his bet with Governor Jennifer Granholm.

MACKINAC ISLAND FUDGE

The origins of Mackinac Island fudge go back to the time when the island changed from the center of the fur trade into a summer resort destination. In the nineteenth century, people enjoyed homemade candy, as national candy makers did not exist, and the Victorian vacationers began to identify the island with sweets. Onto the scene came the Murdick family, and in 1887, they opened the first real candy store on the island, called Murdick's Candy Kitchen. Rome Murdick came up with the idea not only to sell fudge but also to make it on a marble slab in front of the customers and create a show for them as he paddled the cooling fudge. The fudge maker found that making the fudge was as important as the fudge itself, and it continues to be an important part of a visit to the island.

The title "King of Fudge" was given to Harry Ryba. He originally made fudge in Detroit and called it "Mackinac Island fudge" but had never visited the island. In 1960, he and his family set up shop on the island so that his label was legit. Since that time, he has promoted fudge making and business on the island. An interesting spinoff to the fudge story took place in 1986, when Harry and the London's Fair Dairy in Port Huron, Michigan, created the ice cream flavor Mackinac Island Fudge, which instantly became popular. Ice cream companies in Michigan and

Above: Chocolate and ingredients are boiled in a copper kettle, and the aroma attracts customers. *Superior View*.

Right: The marble slab is necessary to paddle the hot fudge. *Superior View*.

Left: Pouring the hot fudge onto the marble slab. *Mackinac State Park.*

Below: The result of the paddling is a loaf of fudge. *Superior View.*

CHOCOLATE CHERRY
CHOC. PEANUT BUTTER
MAPLE
MAPLE PECAN
VANILLA
VANILLA PECAN
BUTTER PECAN

Finally, the loaf is cut in pieces that are ready for sale. *Superior View*.

neighboring states have picked up the flavor, and it is sold in Walmart and the Meijer grocery chain.

The tourist trade all but ceased during the Depression and World War II, and fudge went dormant. Then in the postwar era when the interstate system was developed, Mackinac Island was within easy reach of the visitors who arrived by the thousands during the summer. Today, there are seven fudge makers on the island: original Murdick's Fudge, Joanne's Fudge, Ryba's Fudge Shop, May's Candy Shop, Sanders, Murray Hotel Fudge and Grand Hotel Fudge.

The basic ingredients in the fudge are sugar, unsweetened chocolate, cream, corn syrup, shortening and salt. However, when the vanilla variety is made, it is the first fudge to be heated in the copper kettle to avoid washing the pot. Once the liquid fudge reaches the right temperature, it is poured onto a marble slab and paddled into a loaf as it cools. Then it is sliced at a rate of sixty to eighty half-pound slices in five minutes and is ready for sale.

Fudge making on the island results in approximately ten thousand pounds of fudge or more in a day and has become a multimillion-dollar global phenomenon. Years ago, it prompted one Cold War jokester to say that if Fidel Castro had been able to sell Cuban sugar to the island fudge makers, he would have never turned to Communism. The thousands of visitors—aptly nicknamed "fudgies" by the islanders since the 1960s—are quickly attracted to these shops by the sweet aroma of boiling fudge and the theatrical paddling of the fudge on the marble slab. By far the most popular flavor is chocolate, with its numerous added flavors and nuts, but there is also vanilla and maple fudge. President Gerald Ford is believed to be the only president to visit a fudge shop—May's—when he visited the island in 1975, and he selected vanilla pecan. As many as twenty-nine flavors are available in a season, and experiments are done to develop new flavors, with varying success. Fudge is so popular that some tourists have been known to buy as much as $80 to $100 worth of fudge as souvenirs of their visit. For shoppers, it must be remembered that fudge making is a seasonal industry, but many of the fudge shops have outlets in Mackinaw City, where fudge can be ordered into the holiday season. Whether or not you're on the island, you can celebrate National Fudge Day on June 17.

THE MYSTERY OF THE CUDIGHI SOLVED

The Italian sausage called cudighi was first served in the central Upper Peninsula in the 1930s, having been introduced by northern Italian immigrants. Over the years, this simple food became popular and has developed a near-legendary heritage.

From the start, local food historians have been baffled by the word *cudighi*, as it does not appear in an Italian dictionary, and attempts to try to discover its meaning proved fruitless until 2017, when Laura Gallizioli Young finally provided the answer. Her grandfather Mario Gallizioli, through chain migration, settled in Ishpeming in 1924. He came from Riva di Solto near Bergamo, Lombardy Province, Italy, in the foothills of the Alps. The word *cudeghi* comes from the Bergamasque dialect and was probably the local adaptation of the more standard *coteghino*, a type of sausage. The word has several spellings; Bergamasque dialect is not officially a written language.

According to Gallizioli family tradition, Mario brought the recipe with him, and as Laura tells us, "Our recipe is quite similar to the one you have except my grandfather used 20 percent venison or lean beef in it rather than all pork. Once the family had freezers in which to store the sausage,

Left: Mario Gallizioli (1899–1958), "father of the cudighi," and his wife, Gena. *Laura Gallizioli Young.*

Right: Cudighi sandwiches have been popular since the 1930s. *Author.*

we quit putting saltpeter in, as it was not needed as a preservative." Then Laura concludes, "We use the sausage on pizza, in spaghetti sauce and in sauce over polenta. We also smoke it and serve it sliced with crackers as an appetizer. No one in our family has ever served it with onions or mustard. That must have been an American adaption, as mustard is not used in Italy as far as I know. Our family usually makes the sausage in one-hundred-pound batches, with several families sharing the work and the sausage."

The original story got lost as the Gallizioli family moved to California after World War II. In the early days, cudighi was also a staple enjoyed among North Italian families like the La Frenieres in Ishpeming's North Lake location, unknown to the public. As a result, different families are credited with making the cudighi an iconic food. Felice Barbiere, who was permanently injured in a mining accident and unable to work, was inspired by his family to obtain a recipe, make cudighi in his Ishpeming home and sell it from his shop. Barbiere's fried cudighi, which he always served with mustard and onions on a bun, no matter your taste, quickly became popular among residents, especially next-door taverngoers. The Barbieres later bought a special grill from St. Louis, Missouri, to cook the cudighi and keep the buns warm. After Felice's death, his wife, Yolanda, continued to sell cudighi to high school students, and the popularity of the humble sausage passed to a new generation.

Traditional Cudighi Recipe
from the Family of James La Freniere of Ishpeming

8–12 ounces burgundy wine
2 cloves garlic
25 pounds pork ground coarse, then ground again until it is as fine as hamburger
¾ pound salt (or to taste)
2 teaspoons nutmeg
2 teaspoons allspice
3 teaspoons mace
2 teaspoons cinnamon

Add wine and 2 crushed cloves of garlic to a pot. Bring wine to a boil. Let cool and add to the meat and spices. Mix very well. Then either pump into casings or make patties.
Refrigerate remainder and enjoy.

Onto the scene then came the Gervasi family, who further popularized the cudighi. "My dad had a little white vending truck, and he sold cudighis on two different corners of Ishpeming," said Bruno Gervasi, co-owner of Ralph's Italian Deli in Ishpeming. "He used to go through three or four hundred cudighi a night. It's all my dad's recipe. Homemade bread—if you don't have the homemade bread, you don't have homemade cudighi." Ralph's Deli has been perfecting its recipes since 1964 and has turned the family business into a respected source for a local favorite.

The spices found in traditional cudighi are typical of a sausage from the province of Lombardy in northern Italy. Locally, new generations of sausage-makers have changed the original recipe during the past decade or more. Red peppers and fennel—common to southern Italian cuisine—have been added, and now cudighi can be purchased mild, medium or hot.

Traditionally, the term *cudighi* was only used in Marquette County in the central Upper Peninsula, but today, the term has spread across the region. Restaurants, groceries, meat markets and sausage manufacturers like the Vollwerth Company in Hancock have developed their own recipes. As a result, the term *cudighi* has become synonymous with Italian sausage in the UP. Although it was originally prepared with mustard and onions, it is now served with mozzarella cheese and tomato gravy on a bun or plain, if requested. It is also served on pizza.

CHAPTER 4

Immigrants and Food

BAKERIES AND CONFECTIONERIES

These two businesses with strong ethnic ties are interrelated and evolved into lunch counters and restaurants. This is not to say that native-born Americans were precluded from running such businesses, but for the most part, they were in the minority. Bread was seen as the staff of life, and baking was the second trade in the region after maple sugaring.

Baking bread was an important part of the diet of the early French settlers and military. As a result, they introduced the first outdoor domed ovens at Fort Michilimackinac. A 1749 map shows two bake ovens at the fort, while the Jesuits had their own oven adjacent to their property. There is evidence that in the 1770s, an English baker was paid at the fort. There was a demand for bread by the military at the fort, and hardtack was made for voyageurs and traders preparing for travel. The American posts—Fort Mackinac (1796–1895), Fort Brady (1822–1944) and Fort Wilkins (1844–46, 1867–70)—all followed U.S. Army baking regulations and produced loaves of bread for the men.

As the Upper Peninsula opened to settlement in the 1840s, bakers and confectioners followed. John B. Martell traveled north from Detroit to Sault Ste. Marie and in July 1846 was offering bread, crackers and cakes for arriving vessels and families. Another baker and one of the earliest entrepreneurs was Peter Barbeau, born in Québec. He and others provided bread, rolls, crackers, hardtack and biscuits to the local residents, hotels

The oven was fired up, embers removed and bread added to oven. *Mackinac State Park.*

and passing steamers and would ship orders to the mining regions across Lake Superior.

As the region was settled, the first business to appear in a town was the bakery, which quickly expanded its offerings. In 1874 at Escanaba, Flood & Dodge opened its new bakery and restaurant and offered, besides bakery goods, ice cream, soda water, strawberries and cakes. A.P. Dodge offered bakery goods and confections along with oysters in the dish and can. The People's Bakery provided "meals at all hours."

A number of newly arrived immigrants found that they could make a living with flour, water, salt and yeast. Many Finns and especially Swedes dominated the baking profession across the Peninsula. In 1910 in Calumet, there was a Croatian-Slovenian bakery, and Cameron and Dunlop were Scotsmen who baked in Marquette. In Wakefield, Mircho Dimitroff and Chenco Stoyanoff opened their Bulgarian Bakery around 1914.

Italian bakeries found in many central and western Upper Peninsula communities produced hundreds of loaves of bread a week. Italian

The baker's day usually began at 4:00 a.m., and he had bread and pastries available when he opened at 8:00 a.m. *Superior View*.

Delivery trucks brought baked goods to communities across the UP. *Superior View*.

A typical early Italian bakery. *Superior View*.

Thurner's Bakery in Calumet, 1931. *Superior View*.

households needed frequent deliveries, and in the winter, bakeries like Torreano's in Negaunee delivered bread in charcoal-heated sleds. By the late 1980s, the demand for traditional Italian bread had declined, and the last of the two bakeries producing it—Schinderle Italian Maid Bakery in Iron Mountain and Dante Pricco's Bakery, in business since 1916—closed. The latter was replaced by the Bread of Life Bakery, which challenged the times and continued making Italian bread. On its shelves can be found Italian cookies, such as *biscotti*, *pizelle*, *cialde*, *torchetti* and *grissini*. The late twentieth century saw a new interest in fine food, and new bakeries developed. As a result, saffron buns, limpa bread, ginger cookies cardamom bread and other delights from Scandinavia can be found once again across the Peninsula. Also readily found are specialties such as baguettes, challah, focaccia and *cornetti*. The Trenary Home Bakery was opened in 1928 by Jorma Syrannen, who made twice-baked Finnish coffee bread. Today, it offers a variety of Finnish bakery goods but is best known for its iconic cinnamon toast, Trenary toast, sold in stores and restaurants in the UP. The gigantic cinnamon buns of the Hilltop Café in L'Anse also became legendary with the local public years before such huge buns became popular elsewhere. Small independent pastry shops are opening and making interesting and delicious pastries available. Many of these bakeries have turned to religious holiday items such as paczki, which are popular jelly donuts of Polish origin.

CANDY/CONFECTIONERY

In the nineteenth century, national candy companies did not exist, so there developed a demand for local homemade candy. The first and pioneering confectioner in the UP was Thomas Bendy, an English immigrant who was operating his shop in Ontonagon County in the western UP in 1850. As the decade progressed, confectioneries and their attached bakeries spread across the Peninsula.

In the late nineteenth and early twentieth centuries, homemade candy and ice cream became popular, and Americans and immigrants—Greeks, Lebanese, Italians and Scandinavians—sought to profit from this demand. Confectioneries operated by immigrants, especially Greeks and Lebanese, sprang up across the UP. Many arrived with knowledge of candy making or quickly trained in Chicago and returned to the UP, where they could profitably please the local folk with a variety of candies made from just twenty-five pounds of sugar. Today, two of these enterprises remain in operation: Donckers in Marquette and Sayklly's in Escanaba. Fred

Doncker's original store. *Superior View*.

Doncker's in the 1940s with the candy counter, soda foundation and lunchroom to the rear. *Superior View.*

Donckers arrived from Belgium in 1884 and opened a "news store" in Marquette in 1896 that soon bloomed into a classic confectionery. He made his own chocolates and other varieties of candies, and the soda fountain and restaurant remain popular among residents and visitors alike. The most famous visitor was President Barack Obama, who stopped by for a takeaway lunch on February 10, 2011. He declined the "Obama Burger" with its one-third pound of beef, topped with grilled onions, jalapeños and cheddar cheese, as being "too sloppy" and opted for a house D.J.B. (club sandwich) and a caramel candy. He went on to deliver a pubic speech at Northern Michigan University.

To the south in Escanaba, the Sayklly family from Lebanon opened their confectionery in 1906, and it continues to provide the UP with its well-established candies. Sayklly's endures as the largest non-fudge candy maker left in the Peninsula without an attached restaurant. Its specialties include the ten-pound chocolate bar ("the king of all candy bars"), saltwater taffy and Yooper chocolate bars shaped like the UP, in demand by tourists and former Yoopers living away.

Lindell's Candy and Ice Cream Shop in the 1920s. *Superior View.*

Lindell's crafted interior today. *Author.*

In the Copper Country at Lake Linden, an incredible confectionery from the 1920s, Lindell's Chocolate Shoppe, endures. It was established by Greek immigrants Louis Grammas and James Pallis, who specialized in homemade candy, ice cream and fruits. It was sold to John and Angelo Gekas, who developed a restaurant/soda fountain in 1922. At that time, all of the booths, dark woodwork and fixtures were craft-made, and those classic appointments remain a century later. Lindell's makes a variety of candies and serves breakfast, lunch and ice cream as a piece of living history.

DAIRY PRODUCTS

Dairy products have played a role in the foodways of the Upper Peninsula. The Finns were the most engaged in dairy products, and many of them became dairy farmers. Milk and its byproducts played an important role in their diets. In the old country and the new, they consumed milk (sweet or buttermilk) at most of their meals, whether they ate roast beef, fish or soup. Two products in particular—*viili* and *juusto*—are to be discussed at length, as they were and continue to be part of the diets of third and fourth generations.

The Finns' love of cheese spread to the larger population in Calumet, so stores began to stock both domestic and imported cheeses. In 1896, one store offered gorgonzola, Romano, Swiss, brie and Roquefort, and a bit later, we find Barsotti Bros., an ice cream store, offering Edelweiss camembert, pimiento cheese, potted cheese and D'isigny cheese, a form of brie.

The demand for cheese was quickly met in this cheese-producing paradise. The Upper Peninsula had rich land with abundant grass and diligent farmers who produced cheese. By the 1920s, cheese factories had developed across the region. The cheese produced was primarily American cheese—Colby, cheddar and, beginning in 1923, Swiss cheese. The region became famous throughout Michigan for the fine cheeses it produced, and numerous cheese factories won awards at the Michigan State Fair in Detroit and at the Upper Peninsula State Fair in Escanaba. Unfortunately, beginning in 1950, with transportation costs, need for new equipment, federal health regulations and declining numbers of dairy farmers, dozens of cheese factories began to close.

An example of a Finnish dairy community was Pelkie in Houghton County, where Finns settled between 1900 and 1920. Many of them fled south from

Right: In the early days, butter production was a major project for housewives. *Superior View*.

Below: The Asselin Dairy in Norway, Michigan, left little doubt what it was selling. *Superior View*.

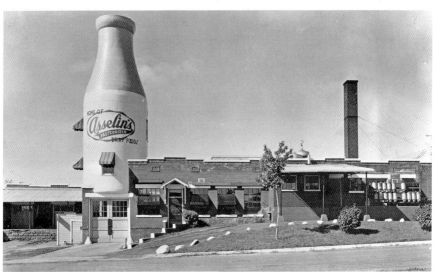

Many Finnish immigrants left mining to develop dairy farms that provided milk for the cheese industry. *Superior View.*

Calumet after the 1913 copper strike, when many were blackballed for joining the strike. The community tied together a number of characteristic elements found in the UP. In 1918, they created the Farmers Co-op Trading Company with 109 members and did $37,800 in sales. A decade later, sales had doubled, and they renamed the business the Pelkie Co-operatives Wholesale Association. By the time it closed in 1995, it included the general store selling food, a creamery and a cheese factory.

Cheese curds are a little-known regional delicacy found in upstate New York, Wisconsin, Minnesota and Michigan, where local dairies produced fresh curds of cheddar cheese that are squeaky when fresh. Today, they are found in cheese stores and groceries, sold under the Sargento Cheese label.

A spinoff food is poutine ("poo-teen"): French fries, cheese curds or regular cheese covered in brown gravy. It originated in Centre-du-Québec in the 1950s and has become popular in the northern United States after entering Michigan through Detroit between 2008 and 2012. Michael and Sonia Stucko introduced poutine to the central Upper Peninsula around 2016, and it is served in many restaurants throughout the Upper Peninsula.

ITALIAN CHEESE FACTORIES

A little-known combination of Italian cheese makers and principally Finnish dairy farmers introduced Italian-style cheese to Americans. Finnish dairymen provided the necessary milk and butter fat to keep the cheese factories operating twenty-four hours a day, and a profitable enterprise resulted. This led to the development of Stella and Frigo Cheese in the Upper Peninsula.

Count Guilio Bolognesi, the Italian consul general in Chicago; his brother Emilio; and their business partner Attilo Castigliano, the Italian consul for the upper Midwest, became involved in the development of a factory in 1917. The count traveled north through Wisconsin and found Lake Nebagamon in Douglas County with an environment suitable for dairy farming. Here, on 1,700 acres, seeing the possibility of making Italian cheeses—Romano, Parmesan, Reggiano and Asiago—he developed a farm. He imported a skilled Italian cheese maker who made Parmesan cheese, which was sold to Italians in Michigan, Minnesota and Wisconsin. Since this and later cheeses were new to the American palate, they had to be tested and his business made solvent. His cheeses were readily bought by Italian immigrants of the western UP who eagerly bought cheeses they had enjoyed in the old country. Originally, they were going to call their product "Nebagamon Cheese," but it quickly became apparent that the name was not conducive to sales. In Italian, "Stella Rosa" referred to high quality, and the new name was adopted.

These new Italian cheeses were introduced to Wisconsin cheese makers and became popular with the American public. As the years passed, the Stella Cheese Company grew with equipment of special design imported from Italy and property acquired not only to make cheese but also to hold it for curing for as long as two years. In November 1929, it dedicated a plant at Mass, Ontonagon County, directed by master cheese maker S. Rossini. It had a capacity of nine thousand loaves weighing twenty pounds each. At the time, it was considered the largest Italian cheese factory in the United States. Citing the Finnish connection, ex-congressman Oscar J. Larson delivered a welcoming address in Finnish, thanking Bolognesi for bringing prosperity to local Finnish farmers. Soon after, plants were opened in South Range, Baltic, Baraga, Crystal Falls, Pickford and Perkins, where they produced millions of pounds of Italian cheeses—Asiago, Caciocavallo, Manteca, Parmesan grated and whole, Parmigiano Reggiano, Provoleta, Provolone, Provolone Fiaschetti, ricotta fresh and dry, Romano, Scamorza and Stracchino. Stella cheese helped many dairy farmers to survive the Depression of the 1930s.

Stella Cheese, headquartered in Chicago, had to pull out of the Upper Peninsula in the early 1950s. This was caused by new and stringent health laws, the need for new equipment, high taxes, transportation costs and diminishing profits and dairy farms. The Wisconsin factories were bought by Universal Foods of Milwaukee, and eventually in 1997, the cheese mega-giant Saputo Cheese USA bought them. That company still sells the Stella brand. It was Count Bolognesi and his Stella factories that brought Italian cheeses to the Upper Peninsula and Wisconsin.

Frigo is another cheese company that originated in Wisconsin along the UP border. Two brothers, Pasquale and Luigi Frigo, arrived in America in 1913. They were from Trissino, Vicenza, north of Venice, home to Asiago cheese. Five generations of the Frigo family had made cheese. By 1920, they were manufacturing Asiago and other Italian cheeses out of Pound, Wisconsin, and were joined by other brothers and developed a number of factories along the Wisconsin border with the UP. In 1939, they incorporated Frigo Brothers Cheese Manufacturers of Iron Mountain. Later, they had a factory in Carney in the UP as well. They eventually had the largest Asiago cheese factory in the United States. In the twenty-first century, Frigo was purchased by Saputo Cheese USA and remains a vital part of the corporation.

SAUSAGE

Sausage was part of all cultures that settled in the Upper Peninsula. In many areas, people kept hogs during the summer, and when the weather grew cold in November, the fattened hogs were dispatched and processed. This was a social event that brought together family, friends and neighbors. The large pieces of pork were usually placed in a crockery jar covered with lard and stored in the basement. Youngsters were sent down to fish out pieces of pork as needed for dinner. The smaller scraps of pork were used to make sausage and the blood turned into blood sausage.

Many of the sausages—blood sausage and head cheese—were common to many of the ethnic groups, but each group had its own special sausages. The Swedish potato sausage was enjoyed by Scandinavians and Finns and was sold in groceries and butcher shops. At one point, near-tragedy struck the potato sausage in 1945, when the Michigan state legislature passed a law that did not allow plant matter to be placed in sausage. Due to outrage from people of all ethnicities who enjoyed potato sausage, the law was quickly changed. We find that the Norwegians had their own potato sausage that added barley and allspice, and the Slovaks in Ironwood had their special potato sausage made with pork, bacon, onions and potatoes. The Finns have their ring bologna called sauna sausage, which is warmed on the sauna stove and eaten as an appetizer with a sauna beer. The Italians had their cudghi, salami and sopresatta.

Given the demand for sausage and the work involved with processing a hog, people turned to local butcher shops that readily filled the demand. In 1910, there were a number of Italian groceries and meat markets producing a variety of sausages and salami. Martin Ciague in Laurium advertised in the Italian Copper Country directory that he was making tasty and delicious packaged sausage, and he also served saloons with their end-of-bar food tables. In 1915, Daniel Holland was not only the postmaster of Hancock but also operated a sausage factory. During the Depression in 1936, "French style blood sausage" and "juicy steaks" were available at the Quality Meat Shop in Sault Ste. Marie, which provided a choice of inexpensive or expensive meats.

German and Bohemian sausage makers during the twentieth century plied their trade across the UP at a time when national companies like Armour and Oscar Meyer were entering the field. Peter P. Wydra, an immigrant from Bohemia, worked for sausage maker Blas Sbimiac in South Range and then moved eastward and opened his own factory, Peter Wydra & Company, in Marquette. In an unusual development, in October 1932, Wydra, who was a stunt pilot, believed that products made in his factory should be delivered as fresh as possible. So he loaded four hundred pounds of sausage in his plane and flew the cargo to Newberry and the Soo. This was probably the first time aerial transport of merchandise from Marquette had been undertaken on such a large scale. He eventually operated two factories in Marquette and the Soo before settling into the Soo Sausage Company and finally the Wydra Food Market. In the 1950s and 1960s, he offered sausage to the delight of Swedes, French Canadians, Italians, Poles and Americans. Steve Melka and Henry Vogeler had smaller factories in Ishpeming serving the central Upper Peninsula.

Walter and Otto Meyer, German Americans from Appleton, Wisconsin, located their sausage plant, Meyer Brothers Sausage, in Ironwood in May 1920. Eight years later, the partnership dissolved when Otto relocated to Caspian. Walter renamed his plant the Meyer Sausage Company and made fifteen to twenty different sausages, including potato, New England style,

Sausage makers at work. Processing machinery is to the right, and the finished product is to the left. *Superior View.*

ring bologna, mince style, frankfurters, pork sausage, Polish sausage, liver sausage, Dutch loaf, braunschweiger, summer sausage, pickle and pimento loaf. Business expanded, and in 1941, Meyer opened a branch plant in Hurley, Wisconsin, immediately to the south. The company served grocers in Gogebic and Iron Counties, as far west in Wisconsin as Superior and south to Wausau. During World War II, the company encouraged housewives to "make ration points go farther" by buying sausage. Today, the plant is no longer in operation.

Otto Meyer opened a meat-processing plant and sausage factory in Caspian that went by the name Meyer Provisions and then Meyer Wholesale, which continues in operation. It produced sausage similar to his brother's company and delivered across the UP and northern Wisconsin. It is best known for the iconic frozen Andy's Steak, renamed Otto's Steak, an ultra-thin steak that takes a minute to fry and is well known throughout the central and western UP.

The most successful sausage maker in the Upper Peninsula was the German immigrant Richard Vollwerth, who started small, developing a sausage factory in the basement of his home in Hancock in 1915. His goal was to make great and quality sausage for the region, which proved a success. By the 1920s, as the demand for his sausage increased, he relocated to a larger, modern and efficient facility and met the demand. During the 1930s, as the Depression forced economizing, he was able to expand because compared to other meat products, sausage is inexpensive and in demand. Over the years, he expanded distribution centers across the Upper Peninsula.

When the Wholesome Meat Act of 1967 was passed by Congress, the Vollwerth Company, now operated by his sons, met the challenge. It won state and national acclaim as being the first meat processor in Michigan to comply with the new law and went on to develop more stringent measures for fine sausage production, an effort recognized by Michiganders. Today, the "King of Meats" fills the demand for an extensive variety of sausage to meet the public need and remains the only major sausage company in the Peninsula.

AFRICAN AMERICANS AND FOOD SERVICE

Nearly since the dawn of settlement in the Upper Peninsula, Black people have been present and involved in food service. After the 1760s, the English kept Black slaves, and in particular, the trader John Askin held Charles, Jupiter Wendell and Pompey, whose labor he used in the fur trade. We do not know if they cooked meals, but there is a strong possibility they did. Jean and Marie-Jeanne Bonga were an enslaved couple taken by the English from the Spanish during a raid on St. Louis in 1782 during the American Revolution. They made Mackinac Island their home, married and operated a hotel/tavern/restaurant.

As the UP opened, Black people found their way north, and in 1850, there were a number of them plying various occupations, like twenty-year-old William Morrsoe at Sault Ste. Marie, who was a cook. An unknown number of Black chefs and waitstaff served guests on steamboats, as on the *Superior*, navigating Lake Superior in the fall of 1854. In 1860, the proprietor of the Mission House, Edward Franks, hired four Black workers: Eliza Smith and Betsy Clayton as cooks and Robert Beasly and Edward Hatton as the waitstaff. At Fort Mackinac, U.S. Army surgeon William Hammond hired two Black servants who provided meals for his family. In 1879, the St. Cloud Hotel on the island had Black waiters in attendance. The employment of a Black waitstaff continued on the island. After the Grand Hotel opened in

The Grand Hotel dining room with Black waitstaff, circa 1920s. *Mackinac State Park.*

1887, it started the tradition of employing Black waiters. Jamaicans have been hired into the twenty-first century as local African Americans have been increasingly less likely to take such employment.

George Preston, born in Canada in 1844, arrived in Marquette in 1865 and became a thriving Black entrepreneur. He owned a barbershop and billiard parlor, and in 1891, he was proprietor of G.C. Preston's Café in the heart of commercial Marquette. His wife, Harriet, possibly managed the café as George continued to operate the barbershop. Eventually, he even opened a confectionery in north Marquette. As a successful businessman, he sent his two daughters, Charlotte and Bessie, to Northern State Normal School to train as teachers.

FINNS AND FOOD

The highest density of Finnish immigrants in the United States—nearly 112,000, or 17 percent of all Finnish Americans—live in Michigan, and the vast majority in the Upper Peninsula, and thus we can best study their traditional foodways. They came to a land similar to the old country and found that they fit into the natural food environment and mingled with other ethnic groups. For instance, the pasty became so popular among the Finns that they believed it was of Finnish origin.

There were berries aplenty, fish, potatoes, rutabagas and dairying—all fit into their diet. Milk and milk products—milk, butter, sour cream, cheese—were more important in the Finnish diet than among non-Finnish immigrants. Many preferred to drink milk (sweet or buttermilk) with their meals, whether it was roast beef, fish or soup. Numerous homes served milk at every meal.

The rutabaga is eaten and cooked by Finns and Finnish Americans in a variety of ways. It is the major ingredient in the popular Christmas dish rutabaga casserole (*länttuläätikko*) served alongside potato and carrot casseroles. The Finns roast, bake, broil and grill rutabagas.

Soups included carrot, cabbage, vegetable and salmon. Fish was always popular and served in a variety of ways: baked, planked, stuffed and stewed. The meats and chicken followed, along with fried frog legs. And then there were the puddings—salmon, liver, rutabaga, corn, rice, bread—that were popular. Herring (*silliä*) was popular, made into puddings and croquettes, baked, salted, pickled and fried. Breads were made with a variety of grains and flour—rye, graham, whole wheat, oatmeal, corn, buckwheat and potato. The most famous breakfast food was the fried or baked pancake (*pännukäkku*). They quickly added maple sugar to their diet along with the local berries that were eaten fresh and preserved as jam.

Two traditional foods were *viili*, a type of clabbered milk, and *juusto*, fresh cheese. The immigrants were aided in their quest for dairy products in small towns where families kept a milk cow until the 1950s. The origins of *viili* go back centuries; it is a traditional food and a way of preserving milk for days. Among Finnish Americans, *viili* is widely known as *fellia*, an Americanization of the very Finnish food. The older generation continues to enjoy *viili*, while the third and fourth generations have turned to store-bought yogurt. *Juusto* is a sweet milk cheese clotted with rennet and is known as "squeaky cheese." It is popular with all generations and can be purchased in stores in the Upper Peninsula.

Since Finns drink the most coffee in the world, this traditional drink was enjoyed in the UP. The older generation in particular enjoys coffee and cake (*käkkukähvi*) served when friends visit. Strong coffee is served accompanied by a variety of sweets, of which a sweet bun (*pulla*) topped with vanilla icing and a sweet bread (*nisula*) flavored with cardamom are popular.

SWEDES AND FOOD

Swedes were another important and large ethnic population in the Upper Peninsula. When they arrived in the UP, they found that the basic items in their diet—fish, cabbage, potatoes, rutabagas and apples—were readily available to them. They were known for their bakery products—limpa and cardamom bread, rusks, hard tack and crackers—provided by immigrant-owned baking companies.

The rutabaga is cooked with potato and sometimes carrot and mashed with butter and blended with stock, milk or cream to create a puree called *rotmos* or root mash. It is often eaten with cured or boiled ham hock or spareribs. Norwegians use it in a similar manner.

The Swedes are also known for Swedish meatballs, potato sausage and headcheese. Apples, an important part of Swedish cuisine, were readily available in the UP and allowed them to make traditional cake, dumplings, pie and pudding. They also made pancakes (*pannkakor*), fruit soup, ginger cookies and carrot pudding.

The traditional smorgasbord was a celebratory meal served buffet style accompanied by beer or aquavit, a potent clear spirit. The smorgasbord was

Superior View.

75

Hallberg and Ostenberg were Swedish immigrants who supplied bakery goods and groceries to Swedish immigrants. *Superior View.*

internationalized at the New York World's Fair in 1939. During and after World War II, the smorgasbord spread to the general population. Various church and community groups began to hold smorgasbords for fundraising events. The House of Ludington in Escanaba in the spring of 1944 had a smorgasbord celebrating "a night in old Sweden." At Marenisco, a "Swedish smorgasbord picnic" was held in the summer of 1949 at the 500 Bushel Club on Lake Gogebic. At this point, the smorgasbord took on a varied flavor when it was incorporated into Labor Day barbecues with a Balkan orchestra entertaining. By 1954, "smorgasbord food delights" included traditional foods but also just about every imaginable food. Swedes complained that almost any varied buffet was called a smorgasbord throughout the United States and in the Upper Peninsula, with good cause.

Although few true smorgasbords were attempted, Chef Pat Hayes of the House of Ludington created the only known elaborate traditional smorgasbord in UP history for Prince Bertil of Sweden in June 1948.

House
Of
Ludington

Caterers to His Royal Highness
Prince Bertil
of Sweden

Presents

The Smorgasbord

SMORGASBORD
Pickled Herring
Fresh Shrimp with Dill
Devilled Eggs
Eggs with Caviar
Liver Pate
Head Cheese
Pressed Jelled Veal
Smoked Tongue
Smoked Salmon

Fruit Soup
Swedish Bread and Sandwiches
Fish in Aspic
Pickled Pigs Feet
Herring Salad
Lobster Salad
Potato Salad
Assorted Fruits & Vegetable Salads
Mixed Green Salad
Pickled Beets
Stuffed Cabbage
Poached Salmon
Boiled Lutfisk
Potato Griddle Cakes
Potato Dumplings
Swedish Beefsteak with Onions

Swedish Meat Balls
Potato Sausage
Fried Potatoes
Baked Ham
Braised Veal Rolls
Roast Pork with Prunes
Roast Duck with Apples and Prunes
Fried Side of Pork
Pork Pancake
Swedish Brown Beans
Mashed Turnips with Pork
Swedish Cheese
Swedish Caraway Cheese
Swedish Brown Cheese
Swedish Pancake with Lingonberries
Rosettes
Poor Man's Cookies
Spice Cookies
Spritz Cookies
Apple Cake with Vanilla Sauce
1000 Leaf Torte
Rice Pudding with Raspberry Sauce

CORNISH AND FOOD

As we have seen, the pasty became the iconic Cornish food for which the UP is renowned. Another Cornish food is kidney pie, whose aroma when being cooked was found to be unpleasant. This has not become an addition to UP dining. Cod, which was replaced by whitefish in the UP, was popular served with dippy, a sauce made with mustard powder. Other traditional dessert foods included saffron buns, a delicious bun made with raisins or currants and flavored and colored with saffron, an expensive spice. Another traditional dessert is seedy cake made with caraway seeds, hence the name. Hevva cake or heavy cake is a lightly fruited cake falling between a sweet scone and a light egg fruit cake and was a favorite in Cornish households. These sweets were served with a smooth yellow cream known as Cornish clotted cream. Unfortunately, aside from the pasty and the saffron buns, these Cornish foods remain only in households and are not found in restaurants or groceries.

ITALIANS AND FOOD

Italian food traditions arrived with the immigrants who settled in the mining regions and at Sault Ste. Marie. The early immigrants found that they could open groceries with little capital, work long hours with family members and eventually develop a profitable business. These stores catered to customers seeking Italian food products such as dried salted cod/baccalà, pasta, polenta, dried mushrooms and olive oil. In Iron Mountain, Michigan, a group formed the Capistrano Mercantile Company. The popular confectionery was found in every community where candy and ice cream were enjoyed. The Italian bakery was an essential business, and warm bread was delivered by wagon directly to homes and boardinghouses in the summer or winter. Between about 1910 and 1930, two Italian pasta factories operated in Hancock, serving a large population.

Besides bread and pasta, Italians enjoyed polenta (much like grits) and served it with stewed meat, fish or chicken. They were also known for capturing and stewing songbirds and rabbits. A popular dish, especially among the Piedmontese and their descendants, is *bagna cauda*/hot bath, a sauce based on anchovy, garlic, olive oil or cream. Savoy cabbage, vegetables or Italian bread are dipped into the thick flavorful sauce. The signature Italian import to American cuisine was pizza, to be discussed later.

Porketta is a traditional dish from the Italian province of Umbria. An authentic version is found at Bimbo's Wine Press (L'Vino Torchio) in Iron Mountain. The dish was pioneered by Bill "Bimbo" Constantini. Porketta is prepared with half a hog, which is salted and peppered, filled with garlic, dill and red peppers and then baked for ten hours. The result is pulled meat with a delicious flavor and crispy outer skin. It is still served on an Italian roll with chips and, if you want to indulge, a beer at the bar.

Italian foods have developed over the years, especially in the Copper Country and the border area with Wisconsin. In 1910, the Copper Country had a population over sixty thousand, and of this number, a third were Italians. As a result, there was a move to meet their food demands. Although pasta—then referred to as macaroni—was sold by national companies, Frank Ricci, a native of Lucca, Italy, opened a macaroni factory in Hancock around 1909. Soon after, planning to return to Lucca, he sold his West Hancock macaroni factory to Pietro Lavorini. In the spring of 1910, Pietro, his son Ferucco and pasta expert Giuseppe Rossi from Chicago were the workforce. The business flourished, and in 1913, it was incorporated. They planned to expand but were stopped by the tumultuous copper range strike. A decade later, Rossi was gone, and Pietro's wife, Maria, joined the workforce at the Hancock Macaroni Company. The factory continued into the 1930s, overseen by Filomena Lavorini, wife of Ferucco, after his death. They manufactured and delivered five- and ten-pound boxes of pasta to immigrant families at their doorsteps. The factory was dissolved, as it was unable to compete with big city macaroni. A second macaroni factory was established in Hancock by Guido Campioni at about the same time, known as the Houghton County Macaroni Manufacturing Company, but was gone by 1930. There were enough Italians in Gogebic County that a macaroni factory opened in Bessemer, but there the macaroni trail ended.

The pasta manufacturers are gone from Hancock and Bessemer. However, Baroni spaghetti sauce, first developed in Calumet in 1935 by Paul J. Baroni, an immigrant from Pisa, Italy, is available. In 2008, the Vollwerth Sausage Company purchased the company and expanded its offerings, which are available online and in stores throughout the Upper Peninsula.

Leonard Scalcucci of Iron River started with frozen pizza in the 1960s and then in 1970 opened Dina Mia Kitchen, producing Italian foods such as pizza, pasta, spaghetti sauce and CheeZee strips. The company sells in the UP, Green Bay and northern Wisconsin. Mamma Russo's Homemade Italian Products is based in West Ishpeming and offers a variety of cudighi, spaghetti sauce and frozen pastas, along with a catering service. For local folk in the central Upper Peninsula, Ralph's Italian Deli in Ishpeming offers homemade Italian sausage and cudighi, spaghetti sauces and packaged imported goods. The Gemignani Italian Restaurant in Hancock has been a culinary landmark for years. In 1999, Tony and Rose Gemignani decided to open Rudy's Traditional Seasonings, seeking to bring their northern Italian recipes to a wider market by offering seasonings for spaghetti sauce, salami, pepperoni, meatballs and the preparation of wild game and jerky.

CROATIANS

Croatians in 1910 numbered 2,536, scattered across the UP but concentrated in Houghton County. They are an example of even a small group leaving a food legacy. In Calumet, they were saloonkeepers, a few merchants and one sausage maker who provided *cevapi* (a sausage seasoned with garlic and paprika) and salami. Between 1906 and 1910, the Croatian Co-Operative was in business supplying ethnic foods. In the

Chickens on the spit are enjoyed by hundreds of Yoopers during the summer. *Author.*

UP, Croatians were at home with wild game—venison, duck, rabbit and goose—mushrooms and readily available dairy products. Today, Toni's Country Kitchen in Laurium is known for its craftsmanship making the Croatian-Slovenian *povitica/potica* or nut roll and is the only shop selling it in the UP, a culinary find for visitors. It also sells other ethnic breads and buns and is famed for its pasties.

Croatian chicken has become part of summer life in the Upper Peninsula. This dish was developed in the early 1980s by Steven Jurkovich and Paul Lucas of Croatian ancestry. Their idea was to share their culture through the vehicle of food. They developed rotating barbecue equipment to mass-produce delicious chickens. Their chicken is available at fundraisers, county fairs and the Upper Peninsula State Fair in Escanaba. Their Croatian Village site is usually surrounded by lines of people waiting for their meal, which includes a baked potato and coleslaw.

RELIGION AND FOOD

The immigrants brought with them not only their foods but also their celebratory use. Finnish immigrants celebrated *Pikkujoulu/*Little Christmas in mid-December at Lutheran church halls or fraternal organizations. It was an informal, highly festive occasion. At this celebration, Christmas dishes were served for the first time. The buffet meal consisted of ham, lutefisk, sausage, potatoes and vegetables and Finnish bread, and the long table was filled with Finnish delights beginning with traditional rice pudding along with fruit soup and a variety of homemade pastries. The most traditional drink was mulled wine. The entertainment consisted of festive speeches, jokes, Christmas songs sung in Finnish and English and then the arrival of Santa Claus/*Joulupukki* with gifts for the children. The Norwegian immigrants had a similar event called *Julebord* with pork ribs, lamb, spicy sausage, lutefisk, sour cabbage, brussels sprouts and lingonberry jam topped off with *glögg* or beer.

Finnish immigrants would also have a dinner either on Christmas Eve or the following day. The traditional menu consisted of beef broth; a tray of pickled fish, cheeses, breads and cold cuts; potato and rutabaga casseroles; beef salad; holiday lutefisk with white sauce; and desserts such as creamed rice spiced with cinnamon and stewed prunes with whipped cream.

The Finns, Swedes and Norwegians enjoy a traditional food, lutefisk, during the holiday season. It is usually dried or salted cod pickled in lye and rehydrated for several days. Then it is boiled and served with boiled potatoes, mashed green peas and bits of fried bacon and covered in a white sauce flavored with spices. It was more popular among Scandinavian Americans than in the homeland and is served at Lutheran church halls and fraternal lodges. Today, lutefisk is not especially appreciated by the offspring of the immigrants.

The Swedish immigrants had *julbord* in the form of an elaborate smorgasbord, which was served as the main meal on Christmas. It consisted of hot and cold foods. The first course was pickled herring and cured salmon, followed by obligatory *julskinka*/Christmas ham, liver pâté, red beet salad and cheese. The third course was meatballs, sausage, pork ribs and cabbage. All of this was washed down with a special Christmas wine. The flood of food on Christmas Day was reminiscent of the celebration after a period of fasting, according to pre-Reformation Catholic tradition, from the beginning of Advent until midnight on Christmas Eve. The other traditional special day was Mardi Gras or Shrove Tuesday, the day before Ash Wednesday, when special buns (*semlor*) flavored with almond paste were baked,

The earliest Frenchmen living at Fort Michilimackinac were known to eat beaver, which they borrowed from the Native Americans. However, the French had to follow the religious dietary restriction of no meat on Fridays or during Lent. The eighteenth-century Finnish chronicler Peter Kalm could not understand the role of fasting as followed by the French. He reported that they "had more courses prepared of eggs, of all kinds of fish, prepared with oils and fats, all kinds of milk dishes, and many especially of sweet and

Typical Little Christmas table. *Author.*

good tasting food than on any other days, and still they called it fasting, *jours maigres* they named them." There is a legendary story that Bishop François de Laval of Québec City asked the pope to declare the beaver, a semi-aquatic rodent and a skilled swimmer, a fish. Much to the delight of the French at Fort Michilimackinac, the pope, as did many zoologists of the time, declared the beaver a fish, and the French were able to dine on the water animal throughout the year.

In the colonial Upper Peninsula, the French Canadians introduced the earliest religious celebrations, which were picked up by later immigrants. They prepared the *tourtière*, or pork pie, for Christmas and New Year. The pies were filled with ground pork, finely chopped onions, ground cloves, allspice and sage. They were made in advance of Christmas and, in the pre-freezer days, were placed in the milk house to freeze. The tradition was for the family to attend midnight Mass on Christmas Eve and then return home, where the *réveillon* (waking) meal was celebrated. This was a special meal that was costly to many of these people who were common workers and did not usually eat in such abundance. The table was set with candles at both ends, and there were cranberries, relishes, oysters on the half shell, creamy pea soup and other items, but central to the meal was the pork pie. Desserts included mashed potato donuts or *réveillon beigne*, gumdrop-nut-raisin cake and pumpkin and other fruit pies. After the grand midnight meal, gifts were opened. On January 6, the Epiphany or "feast of the Three Kings," another celebration, took place and included the king cake, a special coffee cake baked with a bean inside. The person lucky enough to find the bean was considered king or queen for the day and had to present a cake the following year.

Two traditional sweet treats dominated the Cornish celebration of Christmas. Figgy duff, first mentioned in the fourteenth century, was brought to the UP by Cornish immigrants. It is a precursor of plum pudding. The term comes from Cornish colloquialisms: figgy or raisins and duff or pudding. It is baked and is not as rich or complex as plum pudding. It is served with clotted cream. Plum pudding was also a Christmas treat with similar ingredients but was boiled for five to six hours and served with a brandy sauce.

One unique event for early Cornish immigrants was the celebration of Good Friday at the end of the Lenten season. They celebrated the major event of the religious year as Good Friday, the day Christ died, and not Easter Sunday. As a result, Methodist church halls would have large meals that included pasties, singing (for which the Cornish were renowned) and dancing. For instance, on March 21, 1913, the Hurontown Methodist Church above Houghton celebrated Good Friday with a pasty supper followed by a musical program. The other religions were mortified by these celebratory dinners and entertainment. This celebration of Good Friday ended with the last Cornish immigrants and is little remembered. An event developed by the UP Cornish expatriates called the Cornish Connection of Lower Michigan is the celebration of St. Piran's Day, March 5. St. Piran (died circa 480) was a fifteenth-century Cornish abbot and saint of Irish origin who introduced Christianity to Cornwall. On that day, a special luncheon is served with pasties.

Italian immigrants, especially those from southern Italy, celebrated the Feast of the Seven Fishes on Christmas Eve. Fish had to be served, as the eve of Christmas was a day of abstinence from meat. It is unclear why seven fishes were part of this meal, unless there was a connection with the seven Catholic sacraments. The fish were served as appetizers, in salads and as the main course. *Baccalà* or salted cod fish was the basic fish, served in a variety of ways but usually with pasta; there could also be clams and pasta, oysters, deep-fried scallops, octopus salad, stuffed calamari, pasta with anchovies and whatever fish could be purchased.

Italians also had a variety of Christmas sweets depending on the region they came from. Northern Italians, who dominated the mining areas, had *panettone*, a Milanese lightly sweet fruit-studded cake, which is now readily available at Christmas time at Walgreens. The Tuscans centered in Hancock had fruit- and nut-laden *panforte*. The Piedmontese in the Copper Country made nut nougat (*torrone*) and *torchetti* (twisted butter cookies). *Pizzella*, or waffle cookies, usually flavored with anise and baked on an iron form, were popular with all Italians, along with biscotti (double-baked cookie) and fried angel wings or bowtie cookies covered in powdered sugar. Imported chestnuts were roasted and eaten in the evening around the table with a glass of red wine. Cinnamon walnuts were a Christmas favorite among Genovese immigrants.

The Croatians and Slovenians in the Copper Country made nut rolls— called *povitica* (poh-vee-TEET-sah) by the former and *potica* by the latter—at Christmastime. It is a sweet pastry made with a yeast-raised dough; rolled or stretched out thinly; spread with ground walnuts, honey or sugar; and then rolled up jellyroll style in a log or crescent shape and baked in a loaf pan.

Prior to the Lenten season, Polish bakers would make *paczki* (pronounced "POONCH-key")—jelly-filled donuts. This was done so they could use up their supply of sugar and lard prior to the period of fasting, when sweets and certainly lard were not consumed. In the early days, the paczki were homemade, and there was little talk outside the Polish communities of the sweet in the UP. Then in the 1990s, people tasted the paczki, and the demand grew. At first you had to preorder quantities of paczki or arrive at the bakery early in the day because the supply was limited. Today, many bakeries have cartons of them stacked high serving all flavors imaginable days in advance.

The other pre-Lenten pastry is the king cake. This is a sweet bread or coffee cake covered with yellow, green and purple icing into which a baby doll is placed. The person who gets the plastic doll in his or her serving has to buy the next year's king cake. The king cake is probably best known in New Orleans and vicinity, and at first if you wanted one, you had to bring a recipe to a bakery and they would make one for you, or you could order a cake from New Orleans. Yoopers learned of the king cake, and they became popular and are now readily available in bakeries.

At the start of the Lenten season, groceries advertised their Lenten goods. In February 1915, the Fair Savings Bank Department Store in Escanaba listed in two columns the fish available: Holland, smoked, kippered and spiced herring, salted salmon and trout; Norway, mackerel and fish balls, boneless cod and canned fish. The A&P Market in the Soo in 1937 directed shoppers to make the store "your headquarters for fish during the Lenten season." Today, Thill's Fish House, located on the docks of Marquette, advertises its products for Lenten meals, as do other shops across the Peninsula.

Various restaurants like Petrusha's in Ironwood had a fish special every day during Lent, and in 1995, Joe's Pasty Shop in Ironwood offered "gourmet vegetarian pasties."

COOPERATIVES

An important characteristic of food distribution in the Upper Peninsula was and continues to be the cooperative. This was a concept created in Europe and the United States going back to the eighteenth century, but it became popular in the 1890s, when people organized as members of a cooperative so that they would be able to purchase food and other merchandise at a discount and receive an annual monetary return. This idea to counter the corporate domination of the economy was especially strong among Scandinavians and Finns, and as a result, the vast majority of cooperatives were organized in communities home to these ethnic groups.

In the first fifty years of the twentieth century, most UP towns and cities had at least one if not more co-ops. Other nationalities developed cooperative associations. In Calumet, the Croatian community created the Croatian Co-Operative, and the Magyar Co-operative Store and Meat Market opened in Kearsarge. In 1910, the Italian American Mercantile Company of Norway was established and lasted thirty years. Up the road at Iron Mountain, Italian immigrants opened the Italian Cooperative in 1913, and two years later, Italians from the town of Capistrano established the Capistrano Mercantile Company. At Sault Ste. Marie in the spring of 1913, the Soo Co-operative Store opened and eventually grew to three outlets and its own bakery. It advertised its ability to conquer "the high cost of living" and offered fruits, greens, meats and baked goods. There were also occupational co-ops, like the Railway Co-op in Marquette.

The Tamarack Co-operative Store in the Copper Country was hailed as the "largest retail outlet north of Milwaukee" and also one of the most successful co-ops in the United States. Robert W. Bennett, an English

Bakers played important roles in cooperatives. *Superior View*.

Tamarack Cash Market, Calumet, Michigan. *Superior View*.

Interior of the Tamarack Cash Market. *Superior View.*

immigrant familiar with such endeavors, interested John Daniel, general manager of the Tamarack Mining Company, in the idea. It proved that the mining companies could keep wages correspondingly low, as retail prices were low. When the co-op opened in 1890, the board of directors was dominated by mine managers, but as the years passed, the influence of the mine managers diminished. At one point, the store had 6,000 people on its credit books and 125 on its payroll and sales reached $1 million a year.

Many of the UP co-ops closed as mining came to an end and they were no longer seen to be needed. Some of the original co-ops—like Settlers' Co-op, established in 1917 at Bruce Crossing—continue in operation. In the last decades of the twentieth century, a number of co-ops opened dedicated to making healthy food available, including Northwind Natural Foods Company in Ironwood, Keweenaw Co-op in Hancock and the Marquette Food Co-op in Marquette, to highlight a few. The Drifta (Norse for blizzard) Brewing Company located in Marquette is a beer cooperative that opened in 2020.

CHAPTER 5
Beverages in the UP

COFFEE, TEA AND CHOCOLATE

Coffee, tea and chocolate were the first nonalcoholic beverages to enter the UP. The French were fond of coffee and chocolate since they were easily obtained from their South American colonies. It was also shipped from Montréal in sacks or chests, and the coffee was roasted in pans or baked in ovens and then hand ground. Some Frenchmen brewed finely ground coffee similar to thick Turkish coffee. Chocolate arrived in large quantities, was made with water and had sugar and cinnamon and at times an egg yolk added. In 1749, the women at Fort Michilimackinac visited from house to house enjoying coffee and chocolate.

The English also enjoyed *chocolat d'Anglaise*, as the French referred it, with an added egg white. They also used brick tea, easily transported and scraped into a pot or cup. John Askin laid out his beverage problem in April 1778, when the American Revolution disrupted trade to the interior. His wife, Marie-Archange, was reduced to taking tea with loaf sugar once a day, but she would be able to hold out. John and the rest of the family drank chocolate for breakfast and in the afternoon drank roasted barley as ersatz coffee. Otherwise, he had to rely on spirits and locally produced spruce beer.

The chronicles of the explorers and surveyors convey the fact that both tea and coffee were important provisions on their expeditions. With the opening of the UP in the 1840s, it was frequently at a hotel that a "good cup of coffee" was to be found. In 1847, the following were shipped to the Lake

Superior country: green tea varieties gunpowder, imperial and young hyson; black tea varieties lapsang souchong and oolong; and coffee types Brazilian, Cuban, Java and Mocha.

Coffee has remained an important part of life in the UP. The Finnish immigrants thrived on coffee. The Carpenter Cook Company was established in 1891 in Menominee and provisioned communities throughout the UP. The company established the Michigan Coffee & Spice Company and roasted, vacuum packed and sold its product in tins labeled "Wigwam Coffee," "Mi-Lady Coffee" and "Golden Cup Coffee." Today, coffee roasters and shops with names like Dead River Coffee, UP North Roast, Les Cheneaux Coffee Roaster, Superior Coffee Roasting Company and Dancing Crane highlight the land they come from and crisscross the region.

BRANDY, WHISKEY AND WINE

The French brought with them the tradition of drinking brandy distilled from grapes and wine, along with cider. Brandy was not only used in trade with the Indians, but it was also an important part of French life and especially the life of the voyageur. The English who arrived after 1760 continued the tradition, but their favorite spirit was rum distilled from cane sugar found in their Caribbean island colonies. Large quantities of rum arrived at Fort Mackinac, as in 1780, when 1,809 gallons of rum arrived for local use and trade.

When commissioner of Indian Affairs Thomas L. McKenney visited the Upper Peninsula in 1826, he was an alert observer. At the Soo's Fort Brady, he noted the U.S. Army provided the enlisted men with a daily ration of whiskey. Although some of the men were averse to whiskey, they soon adjusted and drank, and some became afflicted with an "inflammatory disease" or became confirmed alcoholics. In 1832, Secretary of War Lewis Cass ended the army whiskey ration; however, Catholic and Protestant missionaries continued to promote temperance among both whites and Native people.

A notice in the *Detroit Gazette* provides a slight insight into the amount of spirits that were being shipped north. Among the four schooners sailing from Detroit to Mackinac Island in early April 1830, they collectively carried 6,700 gallons of whiskey, 1,850 gallons of cider and 5,550 gallons of beer— and this was only the beginning of the shipping season.

As the region opened, warehouses and shops at Sault Ste. Marie were filled with spirits and wines to be shipped west to the mining regions. In 1852, François A. Artault opened the Paris Store at the Soo and offered port, Madeira, sherry, champagne and málaga wines, along with Holland gin and French brandies. He promised for a small commission to obtain and transport any goods and beverages from New York City.

When the mining frontier expanded, visitors wrote of the heavy use of liquor and men making use of the "flowing bowl," which led to gun and fistfights. Some wrote that "there was no Sunday west of the Sault." Jim Paul, "half horse, half alligator," kept his cabin as a public house where the chief entertainments were whiskey and tobacco. Visitors were baffled by the fact that the food supply could be dangerously low, but there was more than an adequate supply of liquor.

Away from the mining frontier in the 1840s, Mackinac Island fishermen developed a new variant spirit, "Indian whiskey," which was considered profitable for fishermen but ruinous to the Indians who traded their fish for it. This "new" product was created "by putting two gallons of common Whiskey, or unrectified spirits, to thirty gallons of water, and adding red pepper enough to make it fiery, and tobacco enough to make it intoxicating." Thousands of barrels were sold annually for fifty cents a quart.

BEER

Beer was the first alcoholic drink to be made in the UP. The Europeans introduced spruce beer, which was made locally, replacing hops with spruce tips. It had a mild alcoholic content. The French were not impressed with it and called it "little beer." It was promoted at Fort Mackinac since it contained vitamin C and prevented scurvy in the troops. However, when the English had the opportunity, they imported ale and porter for the soldiers.

The first German brewers were Nickolas Voelker, Joseph Clemens and Nickolas Ritz, who arrived at Sault Ste. Marie in the late 1840s and had a small brewery operating by the summer of 1850 to serve the local German community. They soon moved to the center of UP settlement with their market in the Copper Country. During the nineteenth century, there were breweries in every large community in the UP. In 1914, there were thirteen breweries in the UP employing some two hundred laborers, mostly European immigrants. Over the decades, they successfully competed with national brands like Budweiser and Pabst. Prohibition ended legal beer production, which never fully revived after 1933. The last brewery—Bosch Brewing in Houghton—struggled to remain open by introducing Sauna beer, to be enjoyed in the Finnish sauna, so popular with Yoopers. Without

Typical beer bottling in the early twentieth century. *Superior View*.

Delivery of Menominee River beer, circa 1910. *Superior View*.

the advertising budget of the national beer giants like Anheuser-Busch, it was forced to close in 1973. However, the brewing tradition has revived. More recently, the first craft brewery, Hereford & Hops, opened in Escanaba on December 7, 1994. Others quickly followed, and twenty-eight years later in 2022, there are twenty-one craft brewers successfully operating across the UP serving the local population and shipping down state and out of state.

DISTILLING

Production of hard liquor is difficult to pinpoint, as it remains undocumented and there was always a generous imported supply available. In 1802, Dr. Francis Le Baron, surgeon at For Mackinac, was using a distillery on the west side of Mackinac Island, but there is no indication of what he was distilling, unless it was medicinal spirits. We know that in 1812 there was an abandoned distillery in Mackinac Island, so there had been at least one attempt at distillation, probably of fermented fruit or berry juice. With the arrival of Italian immigrants, the home distillation of grappa, a potent clear liquor made from fermented grape skins, began, and in some areas, it continues to the present day. Widespread distillation across the Upper Peninsula took place during Prohibition from 1918 to 1933. The first modern legal distillery in the UP, Les Cheneaux Distillers, opened in 2017 in Hessel in the eastern Upper Peninsula. It sells vodka, gin and whiskey under the Straits label.

WINE

European wines were imported and readily available to the colonial French and English, and there is no record of these colonials making fruit or berry wine. Henry Schoolcraft, Indian agent at Sault Ste. Marie in 1834, discussed the possibility of making currant wine in that location, but nothing came of this. In a rare occurrence in 1900 on the Garden Peninsula, which is protected from cold spells, a farmer harvested 233 bushels of grapes and produced fifty-two gallons of wine, while his only UP competitor produced ten gallons of wine.

In the early twentieth century, there was little or no sophistication for European-style wines among the general public in the UP. As a result, at the Christmas season, a liquor dealer at Sault Ste. Marie offered a variety of sweet wines: port, sherry, blackberry, muscatel and orange. The Catawba and Scuppernong were East Coast wines known for their distinctive musky wild flavor, which was not attractive to the immigrants.

Italians, Croatians, Slovenians, French Canadians and other wine-drinking immigrants were not attracted to the American-grown grapes. When they found that it was near impossible to cultivate grapes in the UP, they took action. They contracted with local agents to have rail cars arrive filled with grapes from California, New York and Ohio, and winemaking began. Each man made two hundred gallons of his best wine for his family and more if they took in boarders. Traditionally, the wine was tasted with ceremony on November 11, St. Martin's Day.

During Prohibition, individuals were allowed to make two hundred gallons of wine annually to be consumed by the family. Anything over that amount got you into trouble. California vintners had a dilemma, as they could not sell their grapes to wineries. They survived by selling grape bricks—dried grapes formed into bricks with such labels as "Santo Vino." The bricks arrived in the UP with a wink-and-nod warning on the cover: "After dissolving the brick in a gallon of water, do not place the liquid in a jug away in a cupboard for twenty days because then it would turn into wine." Burgundy, sherry and port flavors were also available.

Although the immigrants were unsuccessful growing grapes because of the short growing season, the University of Minnesota has developed varieties of cold-hardy grapes that have allowed local vineyards and wineries to flourish. As a result, a number of vineyards and wineries have emerged in the southern UP: Leigh's Garden Winery (Escanaba), Northern Sun Winery (Bark River), Threefold Vine Winery (Stephenson) and Garden Bay Winery (Cooks). A number of other wineries use grapes either from lower Michigan and elsewhere.

Not all of the operations use grapes for their finished product. In Greenland in the western UP, there is the only meadery in the region, Algomah Acres Honey Meadery. The Barrel & Beam in Marquette has developed a number of varieties of cider. The End of the Road Winery in Germfask makes two curious Yooper wines: Happy Sap, made from local maple syrup, and Tahqua Rush, made from farm rhubarb.

SALOONS

With the arrival of the Americans came the saloons, but it must be emphasized that these saloons also served as early restaurants. As Louis

Saloons were centers of food and drink where men socialized around billiards. *Superior View*.

Patrons enjoying a round of beers. *Superior View*.

Agassiz noted in the summer of 1848, "The most striking feature of the place [Sault Ste. Marie] is the number of dram-shops." Standing in front of his hotel, he counted 7 saloons along with "larger stores" that only sold liquor. Over the years, wine and spirits by the thousands of gallons entered the UP to quench the thirst of Yoopers. In 1907, sixty years after the frontier opened to settlement, there were over 1,000 saloons scattered across the land, which equals 358 saloons for every man, woman and child living in the UP. The copper towns of Calumet and Laurium had 114 saloons, to serve 17,000 people or 1 saloon for every 137 citizens. This thirst continued until state and national Prohibition began in 1918 and 1920, respectively, which had the effect of lowering the number of taverns that grace the cities and dells today.

CHAPTER 6

Restaurants

TOURIST ORIGINS

The pursuit of a meal in the wilderness of the Upper Peninsula successfully evolved beginning in the early nineteenth century. During this evolution, dining habits and types of food consumed have been influenced by society and the economy and altered as well. Understanding these developments allows for an appreciation of restaurants in the twenty-first century.

The evolution of the Upper Peninsula's restaurant culture had its inception at Sault Ste. Marie and Mackinac Island as tourism replaced the fur trade. The incoming folk arrived seeking to enjoy the beauty of the region, and in an era without air conditioning, visitors fled the hot and humid South, where deadly malaria and yellow fever festered, to seek the cool summers of the North. How best to enjoy the stay with good meals?

As early as the 1790s, small numbers of people braved the trip to Sault Ste. Marie to gaze in awe at the immensity of Lake Superior and its azure waters. These early visitors either brought their own food—salted pork, bacon, flour, coffee—or relied on the hospitality of Native Americans and early settlers. Finding the brisk summer air and the environment invigorating, they spread the word to visit the area for health and pleasure.

We are fortunate to have an intimate account of how one of the early visitors to the Upper Peninsula wilderness dined. The commissioner of Indian Affairs, Thomas McKenney, arrived at the Soo during the summer of 1826 and encountered a village of 152 people served by a bake house, two groceries and the government larder at Fort Brady, where food could be purchased—the last point of civilization at the entrance of the Lake Superior frontier.

McKenney found the basic fare was whitefish, brook trout, lake trout and potatoes, along with a variety of locally grown vegetables and the use of maple sugar as flavoring, which Native people, Métis and French Canadians were fond of. During his short stay, he dined with the officers at Fort Brady and with Indian agent Henry R. Schoolcraft and his Métis wife, Jane, who opened their home to him as they did to other visitors. When he dined with the Johnston family, the Irishman John and his Ojibwa wife, Ozhaguscodayway, McKenney was greeted with "genuine Irish hospitality," and the home was "a place of most agreeable resort to travelers." He also found the women's culinary skills to rival those of chefs in Washington, D.C.

White visitors frequently relied on the hospitality of Native Americans, as restaurants were lacking in this remote region. When early white settlers arrived at the future site of Marquette in 1846, they were greeted by the Kawbawgam family and other Native Americans. At the Kawbawgam Hotel, Charlotte Kawbawgam served them a meal of boiled and fried whitefish, "unequalled potatoes," fried venison and good coffee and bread. In 1852 near Baraga, Wimtogoshine, an Ojibwa elder, served broiled trout, sweet ham, hard bread and coffee to visiting fishermen who concluded, "We recollect few dinners with as much satisfaction and pleasure."

The first restaurants developed at Sault Ste. Marie at the gateway to the Lake Superior country in the form of hotels and saloons. In July 1846, Langley and M'Donald's Bowling Saloon and eating house provided meals and "a cup of good Coffee and other refreshments at all hours." A year later, Messrs. Stevens and Cornwall oversaw the Ste. Marie Hotel, "unsurpassed northwest of Detroit." Stevens had formerly been a steward on the "floating palaces" that traveled the lakes and came with a solid reputation, as seen with the announcement that "no expense or attention shall be spared in furnishing the larder at all times with the choicest articles that can be provided." Fishermen could fish the waters of the St. Mary's River and dine on their catch prepared by a local chef.

An anonymous tourist-author signing himself merely as "S.S.S." left a detailed account of his culinary experience at the Ste. Marie Hotel in the late summer of 1847. The day started with a "well-filled breakfast table" before touring the town. At 1:00 p.m., he "sat down to a dinner which would have done justice to any hotel this side of New York." A staff of waiters elegantly served a well-prepared meal. The piece de resistance was the "dainty morsel

A typical nineteenth-century waitstaff. *Superior View.*

of the epicure, the *brook trout*, served up *decidedly* in the best style possible!" He ended his review encouraging any who visited the Soo to dine at the Ste. Marie Hotel, but all of the proprietors sought to provide visitors "still within the pale of civilization and refinement" with a fine dining experience.

Fifty miles to the south, Mackinac Island was experiencing the arrival of tourists as well. Many of the early visitors who arrived at Mackinac Island were prominent and wealthy individuals and families there for their health and sightseeing. Having arrived by ship, they stayed for weeks and months in the summer in small hotels whose proprietors, many of whom were women, provided them with fine dining.

These guests were of national and international importance. In 1834, Captain Tchehachoff, a member of the Russian Imperial Guard, arrived, as did Secretary of War Lewis Cass, who visited with his daughter. The Austrian and Sardinian envoys traveled north to avoid Washington, D.C.'s hot and humid summers. In 1848, Illinois congressman Abraham Lincoln and his wife, Mary, on their way home to Springfield, Illinois, from a New York political tour, made a hurried stop at Mackinac. While the *Globe* loaded wood and provisions, they visited the sights and probably had a meal or tea before continuing their voyage.

By the 1840s, steamboats brought luxuries of the South—fresh and succulent fruits and vegetables—supplemented by nearly one hundred local farmers who provided highly regarded local potatoes and other crops and by many fishermen who provided an endless supply of near-legendary lake trout and whitefish. As the decade of the 1850s proceeded, the hotel ventures increased, and the keepers sought to provide an "at home food and beverage experience." M.M. Gillett operated the Lasley House in 1851, and a year later, Edward A. Franks, proprietor of the newly expanded Mission House, "now one of the largest and most extensive establishments in the country," planned "to spare no expense in making the Mission House a pleasant resort for those who visit the Island in search of health and pleasure." At the neighboring Huron House on the island, the proprietor stressed, "No effort shall be wanting to promote the comfort and happiness of the guests." In 1855, the five larger hotels, with their splendid dining rooms, along with the twenty to thirty smaller hotels could not keep up with the influx of guests

The Superior Hotel (1891–1929) was built overlooking Marquette with twenty rooms, a sanatorium and a dining room catering to tourists and hay fever sufferers. *Superior View.*

to the island, and without reservations, visitors were forced to return to the vessels that brought them and begin the long trip home. As a twenty-first-century observer noted, "People don't come to Mackinac Island for hamburgers but for delightful dining."

In the 1850s and 1860s, more prominent people visited the island. In August 1853, Archbishop Cajetan Bedini, nuncio of the Papal States, and Archbishop John Hughes of New York City stayed and dined on the island. The island was also visited by ex-president Millard Fillmore and Henry David Thoreau, who was seeking relief from tuberculosis, along with others.

As the copper and iron regions opened and developed, not only was there transient traffic to the mines, but tourists also arrived to see the developing mines and mills. Traveling across the vast expanse of Lake Superior, tourists found that the stewards aboard ships like the *Independence* provided outstanding dining service. Once they arrived in the Copper Country, they could relax and dine at Hiram Joy's Eagle Harbor House or the Brockway House at Copper Harbor, where every effort was made to make them feel like they had not left "civilization." Similar culinary developments took place at Marquette. By the summer of 1851, a year after the village was created, A.N. Barney had opened the Carp River House, followed by others, and eventually in the 1860s, the Northwestern Resort on the shores of Lake Superior offered accommodations and dining. Generally, visitors were never beyond the reach of fine dining.

THE RESTAURANT EMERGES

Dining possibilities further expanded, and no longer were hotels and saloons the only places to dine. In 1862, while the Civil War raged to the south, H.F. Stanton, proprietor of the Alhambra restaurant in Marquette, offered fresh oysters, brook trout, wild game "and other edibles too numerous to mention, which he gets up in a style that would tempt the palate of an epicure." His bar "accommodations are unsurpassed by any other establishment on Lake Superior." The restaurant O.K. Hall, also in Marquette, kept "constantly on hand the finest oysters, pigs feet, wild game, tripe and all the delicacies of the season."

One of the earliest and most legendary hotels in the Upper Peninsula was the Hotel Ludington or, as it has come to be known, the House of Ludington in Escanaba. It opened in the 1860s as the largest hotel north of Milwaukee

Many women found employment as waitresses. *Superior View*.

and became well known for fine dining for both local residents and visitors from Chicago and points south. In the late nineteenth century, when most restaurants catered to the short-order trade, the hotel offered fine food and impeccable service. In the 1880s and 1890s, it was not uncommon to serve venison and duck that the chef bought directly and processed locally.

House of Ludington, 1911. *Superior View.*

A July 1893 menu shows delicacies the hotel provided its guests—baked lake trout with fine herb sauce; tenderloin of beef larded with French peas; roast sirloin of beef au jus; spare ribs of pork with brown potatoes; potage de la reine/Queen's soup; boiled beef tongue with pickled sauce; roast leg of veal with jelly; lobster salad; fricassee of chicken with mushrooms; and ending with a choice of desserts: Charlotte of fruit with Galantine brandy sauce, English plum pudding and, at last, lemon ice cream, American and Edam cheese, Imperial Punch, coffee and iced tea. The culinary reputation of the House of Ludington was continued by legendary owner and chef Pat Hayes. He was known for creating elaborate themed culinary events beginning in 1939 and lasting for thirty years. Under his direction, the restaurant gained a national reputation and hosted governors, senators, industrial and business leaders and television personalities. (More about him in the last chapter.) It was considered a showplace of the Midwest. Today, the House of Ludington continues as the cornerstone of Escanaba and retains its culinary tradition of specializing in fish.

In the 1870s, other hotels in Escanaba offered fine dining. David Oliver, proprietor of the Oliver House, provided "a well-kept table for guests," while the Tilden House pastry chef, Mr. Robinson, was showing a fine specimen of his work at the Flood & Dodge bakery.

Bakeries and confectioneries were the first to pioneer restaurants or lunch counters for day workers across the UP. As a working example, we can look at restaurant developments in Escanaba in the 1870s. Bakeries began to serve as restaurants, offering "warm meals at all hours." Frank Baker operated a "first class restaurant" where he offered fine fish, anchovies, rolled and sour herring, many varieties of cheese and fresh oysters, game and poultry in season. Confectioneries were offering ice cream and soft drinks, and some of them promoted themselves as "temperance halls."

By the early twentieth century, Sault Ste. Marie had attracted a variety of foreign restaurant proprietors. Greeks tended to dominate the food scene. In 1910, James Nanos and Frank Kristselis, two Greek immigrants, sold homemade candy and ice cream in their confectionery, the Superior Candy Kitchen, and soon added a dining hall, Red Star Restaurant. They offered ice cream treats, short-order lunches at all hours, regular meals for $0.15 and above and monthly meal tickets starting at $3.50. They took pride in

Khoury's soda fountain, Iron Mountain. *Superior View*.

their food enterprise and frequently enlarged, remodeled and redecorated the premises. The Manhattan Restaurant had a "dining hall for ladies and gentlemen." John Skourouhos had the European Restaurant, which in addition to shelf groceries, confections and fresh fruit and vegetables also offered meals and short orders at all hours. The Olympia advertised that it pioneered "strictly pure ice cream" and had "the finest appointed refreshment parlor in the North." Around 1907, two Japanese men, Jutaro Ichii and Ken Suzuki, operated the Togo Restaurant and catered to the public with $0.25 turkey dinners. Frank G. Oster (1875–1959), a Swedish immigrant, operated a restaurant and lunch wagon in the Soo. He was highly innovative, catering to men and women, using fresh poultry and oysters and offering waffles on the menu when the electric iron arrived. In 1922, he introduced the "Coney Island Outfit," the first device in the UP for making sandwiches.

Service and dining attitudes were changing. In 1916 in the Soo, the Parisian Restaurant and its bakery supplemented service with a Dairy Lunch Room preparing steaks and chops in fifteen minutes and had quick lunches to take out. Focusing on locally produced foods, it offered "Cloverland" chicken, turkey, duck and strawberries, along with fresh oysters and shrimp from the East Coast and fresh frog legs. Sunday dinners were advertised as enjoyable, restful and economical, and housewives should "give up the tiresome work of getting meals and try eating here every day." In the heart of the Depression in 1936, Kay's Cocktail Lounge and Restaurant in Marquette offered a "Special Sunday Dinner served from 11:30 a.m. to 8 p.m."

Kay's Cocktail Lounge & Restaurant
September 27, 1936

Fruit Juice Cocktail   Cream of Tomato-Old Fashioned
Broiled Lake Superior Trout–lemon butter
Baked Young Turkey—dressing--apple sauce
Roast Prime Ribs of Beef—au jus
Small Blue Ribbon T-bone Steak, maitre d'hotel
Snowflake Potatoes   Shoestring Potatoes
Mashed Rutabagas   buttered green beans
Cuban Salad
Raisin Pie, Peach Pie, Angel Food Cake ala mode
Choice of beverages

The Margi Grill in Munising, 1950, when the jukebox reigned. *Superior View.*

With this assortment of choices available for sixty cents (eight dollars today) per plate, many people began to appreciate the value of restaurant dining. However, the day of the drive-in and the fast-food restaurant was far off on the horizon for now.

Since the opening of the UP, food providers were concerned about making the best food and service available. In the 1840s, the best stewards on steamers were hired away by newly opened hotels because of their skills serving diners. Later, restaurant proprietors raided chefs from across the UP or imported them from urban centers to provide quality dining experiences similar to those in Chicago.

ETHNIC RESTAURANTS

Chinese Restaurants and Chop Suey

Despite its rural setting, the Upper Peninsula was cosmopolitan in the development of its ethnic restaurants. Even in the faraway corner of the UP, Chinese restaurateurs found they were at home with limited competition. In October 1897, Chang Yeng returned from San Francisco, where he received culinary training, and opened one of the first Chinese restaurants in the UP at Calumet. At the Soo in 1911, Wah-Hing-Lo's Chop Suey Restaurant served Chinese American food and was open all day until 2:00 a.m. By 1915, Charlie Sam had a restaurant in Hancock and Howard H. Chinn operated the Oriental Grill on Shelden Street in Houghton, offering Chinese and American food. The 1920s saw Chinese restaurants spread across the UP, such as the Oriental Café that opened in Marquette for a short run, and in Escanaba, Charles Chow and Edward Wong served the public. At the same time, Charles Lee opened the New Hong Kong Chop Suey House and Restaurant in Ironwood, whose interior was renovated and booths installed complete with Chinese decorations.

Coinciding with the growing popularity of Chinese restaurants, a chop suey craze hit the United States and the Upper Peninsula. As with popular foods and drinks, its origin has entered mythology, and this Chinese American dish is unknown in China. The food was considered "exotic" by Yoopers, but the dish was easily made with simple ingredients—a mixture of pork/beef/shrimp, vegetables, starch thickener and rice. By the first decade of the twentieth century, chop suey restaurants appeared from Calumet to Sault Ste. Marie.

The development and opening of the Chop Suey Café, the first in Escanaba, in November 1922 is a good example of the popularity of the dish and illustrates how Greek immigrants became involved in chop suey. Gus Graphos, owner of the Candyland Store, decided to make a change and open the first chop suey restaurant in Escanaba. He sent a manager to Chicago to study Chinese restaurants, and a Chinese chef was brought north. The candy shop was redecorated with Chinese lanterns and cherry blossoms, providing an "Oriental atmosphere." For the opening and subsequent evenings, music was provided by Johnson's or Le Duc's Orchestras, and room was made for dancing. For Thanksgiving, Graphos offered noodle soup, olives and a choice of turkey chop suey or chicken chow mien with fried noodles, topped off with oolong tea and kumquat preserves. Within a month of opening, the Chop Suey Café was offering take-home chop suey by the pint or quart.

The popularity of the dish grew. It was served at home parties, lodge halls, church bazaars, meetings and student athletic gatherings. At home, people could have "fun" with chopsticks and dress in appropriate Chinese clothes creating "Chinese hospitality" as they enjoyed their chop suey. By 1924, when the Chinese tile game of mahjong swept the country in popularity, UP newspapers promoted the idea of the party giver to "cook Chinese" and serve chop suey. Newspapers provided recipes for the unknowing.

As the chop suey craze ended, a downward economic spiral set in. The Depression closed mines and mills; there was a revival during World War II, but the postwar years saw the UP economy in trouble. However, it soon bounced back as new techniques revived iron mining; medical facilities expanded along with universities; skiing and other sports were promoted; and two airbases, Kincheloe AFB at the Soo and K.I. Sawyer AFB south of Marquette, opened. A rather cosmopolitan population emerged that sought new dining experiences.

In 1974, the Tai Long, the first restaurant serving Chinese cuisine north of Green Bay, opened in Marquette. Since that time, Chinese, Japanese and Thai restaurants are to be found in all of the major communities in the UP. In Marquette, the tiny and unassuming Rice Paddy serving Thai food gained a reputation in faraway Washington, D.C. When President Barack Obama visited Marquette in February 2011, his staff headed for the Rice Paddy for lunch.

Italian Restaurants

The second-most popular restaurant in the United States is the Italian restaurant, which is also found in UP communities with a large Italian American presence. In the first decade of the twentieth century, the Copper Country, with its sixteen thousand Italians and numerous Italian colonies, saw the début of Italian restaurants. In Calumet, Maurizio Bandettini operated the Michigan Hotel with its buffet and café offering food and imported wine and liquor. The Columbus Restaurant and Saloon was advertised as "the most famous establishment in Calumet where friends and countrymen meet for food and drink." There were a half dozen Italian-owned saloons that served counter food and buffets. To the south in Houghton, Antonio Giuglio was the proprietor of the Torino Hotel, the only Italian hotel in Houghton County. Giuglio offered Italian dining and special rates for wedding and baptismal luncheons.

Across the UP, restaurants owned by Italians began to appear in the first half of the twentieth century. During the 1920s, Hugo Baroni of Calumet opened his restaurant, and by the early 1930s, Perotti's Italian Restaurant in Bessemer was offering its popular ravioli and "other Italian dishes daily!" In June 1933, members of the Bessemer Business Men's Association were "served heaping plates of spaghetti and chicken." Down the road in Jessieville, Giannunzio's Italian Restaurant was offering "Special Saturday Homemade Spaghetti."

Steaks in preparation.
Superior View.

Three interesting tavern-restaurants located in Ishpeming commemorated the end of Prohibition in 1933. Joseph Nardi opened the Senate Café, Joseph Gagliardi established the Roosevelt Café and A. Louis Bonetti held forth at the Congress Bar & Café. The Senate has long been closed, while the Roosevelt was a hangout for the cast and crew when *Anatomy of a Murder* was being filmed in town in March–April 1959. The actors could come in at any time and order steaks cooked by the owner, "Gigs" Gagliardi. Although it is no longer a bar, you can visit the establishment—now Globe Printing—and go to the basement and see the wall of autographs of the cast and crew of the movie. The Congress has survived as a bar and restaurant and is known for its pizza, cudighi sandwiches and pizza fries, attracting locals and people from afar.

Although Italian restaurants had gotten their start, the end of World War II really began the development of Italian restaurants in earnest. Yooper veterans who had served in Italy and were familiar with Italian food were eager to enjoy the cuisine with their families. The taste of garlic, oregano and wine were all new experiences for many Yoopers, who were moving from bland white food to one of bright orange-red garlicky sauces and strangely shaped pastas. It did not take long for Italian restaurants to open across the UP and just across the state line at Ironwood in the Italian American enclave of Hurley, Wisconsin. In 1949, De Masi's Spaghetti House in Ironwood was offering spaghetti and meatballs or chicken made with "home-made noodles" for seventy cents and sixty cents, respectively. The Italian restaurant that emerged in the UP has a typical cuisine: spaghetti, ravioli, gnocchi, lasagna, rigatoni, minestrone soup, prime rib, steaks, chicken, shrimp, "buttery" garlic rolls and traditional pizza.

Pizza had its roots in Naples, Italy. During the 1950s, it quickly became the mainstay of diets throughout America and the Upper Peninsula and is the ultimate popular Italian food. Early mention of "pizza" appeared in articles

Pizza preparation at the Congress. *Superior View*.

in the *Ironwood Daily Globe* in 1935 discussing pizza in New York City. A decade later, the same newspaper carried an article on how to pronounce the new food: "PEET-zah." Further educating the public, the article continued that pizza was an "Italian pie with a savory filling usually made of sausage or anchovies and cheese" and it was "the after-the-movies snack favorite of teen-agers." The article provided a recipe.

Suddenly, you could enjoy a pizza at a tavern while watching "all important sports events telecast." On Fridays and during Lent, Catholics could enjoy non-meat pizzas. New Year's Eve parties were ending with a "hot pizza lunch." Pizza burgers and pizza pasties appeared on menus. In Escanaba, Marco's Restaurant in 1957 was offering "hot pizza—delivered free," an innovation that was spreading. Pizza became popular with teenagers and was served at school lunches, parties and home meals. In 1964, Rossini's Restaurant in Sault Ste. Marie had "Pizza Day for Students" and offered "a wide assortment" of toppings and a one-third discount for teenagers. On the grocery shelves, Chef Boy-ar-dee had pizza pie packages ready for home baking, and frozen pizzas were an option. In 1957, at Pickford in the eastern UP, as part of a fundraiser, members of the Future Homemakers of America were available to come to your home for odd jobs, which included "making pizza pie." By the late twentieth century, local pizza outlets were well entrenched and continued to flourish with the arrival of national chains.

Scandinavian Restaurants

Restaurants serving complete Finnish meals are nonexistent in the UP. However, in the Copper Country, two restaurants that serve primarily midwestern food also offer pasties and Finn-related foods. The Kaleva Café opened in 1918 in Hancock and serves oven-baked pancake (*pännukäkku*) and Finnish French toast. In Houghton, the Suomi Home Bakery and Restaurant offers Finnish French toast, cinnamon *nisu*/toast and *pännukäkku*.

A small variety of foods from Finland are found in A Touch of Finland in Marquette. Besides the Finnish mustards and candy, especially salt licorice, there are bags of what Finns thrive on: coffee from Finland. Cinnamon toast—Trenary toast—is available through the Trenary Home Bakery and is a popular part of the local cuisine available throughout the Upper Peninsula.

In Escanaba, home to a large Swedish American population, the Swedish Pantry with its gold and blue façade is found on Ludington Avenue. It serves Swedish American midwestern cuisine. Of special note are its Swedish pancakes, served with lingonberry jam; Swedish meatballs; and fries. It is decorated with items that give the diner a taste of Sweden. The attached bakery prepares large cookies and cinnamon buns along with cardamom bread and limpa.

Other Unique Food Experiences

German food entered the Lake Superior region in the late 1840s, when German immigrants settled at Sault Ste. Marie. Later, in the 1910s, the Deutsch Haus served traditional German food. Marquette has had a number of traditional German restaurants since the 1960s: Tiroler Hof's Red Eagle, the Bavarian Inn and most recently the Stein Haus. However, German food can be found in a number of restaurants across the Peninsula. The Mexican restaurant, with hot, spicy food, was slow to enter the UP, beginning in Iron Mountain in the 1970s. Mexican food has been readily accepted with all of its usual hot foods and sauces, which comes as a surprise to many. Today, at least one Mexican restaurant is found in every major community in the UP. In Marquette, Lagniappe Creole and Cajun Food comes as a surprise this far north, serving authentic New Orleans food and drink; it has been joined by the Court Yard. Finally, Buhadin Kahn, a native of Afghanistan, settled in Calumet prior to 1925 and opened a chili restaurant. He later moved to Iron Mountain, where he continued to serve chili to eager patrons. He was known throughout the UP as "the king of chili makers."

Two restaurants in the Copper Country have unique charms. The Michigan House Café & Brewpub in Calumet was operated by the Bosch Brewing Company. In 1906, the company had the Milwaukee Artists' Alliance create a large ceiling mural depicting a happy, brew-filled picnic. The mural survived Prohibition and smiles down on customers today. The Ambassador Restaurant in Houghton has murals lining the walls. Joseph Bosch commissioned Milwaukee artist Franz Rohrbeck to paint oil-on-canvas murals depicting elves in various states of celebration. During Prohibition, the murals were rolled up and put in storage, and they came out again in 1933. In both cases, they are possibly the only two examples of this type of art created for brewery saloons in the state of Michigan.

PRIVATE CLUBS

As the Upper Peninsula developed, there was a growing demand by the local businessmen and entrepreneurs for private clubs where they could relax around fine food and drink—an environment not previously available to them. The oldest private club in the Upper Peninsula was the Le Saut de Sainte Marie Club located at Sault Ste. Marie, organized in 1887 with membership consisting of businessmen, attorneys, engineers with the Soo Locks, physicians and insurance agents. At a meeting of the board of directors in March 1888, it was decided to add a restaurant. S.R. Snow of the Hotel Iroquois became the steward. The dining room was well furnished, and service was considered elegant. When the club was formally organized in October 1889, it possessed spacious parlors and a banquet hall in the Savings Bank Building in Sault Ste. Marie. Meals were usually topped off with special speakers, and during the winter season, members and guests of the club attended a series of card parties and dances accompanied by collations or suppers.

The club frequently hosted meals and buffets for visiting congressional delegations, Michigan gubernatorial visits, the Commercial Club, the curling club and city organizations. In August 1894, an elaborate reception was held for the Knights Templar and their guests. After the hop, at midnight, chef Anthony Neary presented an elegant repast whose menu has survived. It consisted of sardine sandwiches, "ham garnish," buffalo tongue, roll breast of veal stuffed, several salads and desserts consisting of champagne jelly; walnut, sponge and chocolate cakes; three ice creams topped off with fruits; and candy and coffee. The club continued to provide food and entertainment for its members and guests into the dark days of World War II. With the arrival of ten thousand troops to guard the St. Mary's River Canal, life was disrupted, and the club ceased to exist.

The Marquette Club was organized by elite businessmen in 1889. It started as a literary society and then changed to a social club. Light luncheons to receptions featuring champagne punch, cake and coffee were held. The club lasted until the late 1970s.

During the copper boom, Calumet was one of the larger cities in Michigan. The substantial professional staff of mining presidents and captains, owners and operators, businessmen, bankers, physicians and lawyers needed a private dining club. This was accomplished on July 1, 1903, with the opening of the Miscowaubik Club. It became the gathering place for the wealthy and consisted of very elegant surroundings: billiard, dining, reception, card and bath rooms; lawn tennis; indoor golf; and world-class cuisine and impeccable service. It was the "most modern and exquisite taste" of the day.

Miscowaubik Club
Calumet, Michigan
November 26, 1909
32nd Degree Masons of the Copper Country

Canape de Caviar
Olives   Celery
Puree of Green Peas au Croutons
Fillet of White Fish
Philadelphia Squab encrusted with Parisian Potatoes
Wax Beans a la Miscowaubik
Roman Punch
Grape Fruit   French Dressing
Leptour Cheese
Ice Cream   Assorted Cakes
Demi Tasse   Cigars

The tradition continues to the present. The club is supported by annual membership and still offers the same amenities and world-class cuisine enjoyed by the privileged few during the boom days. It is one of the best-kept secrets of the area.

The Crystal Falls Club was formed by local businessmen. By the spring of 1914, they were holding regular weekly luncheon meetings. Besides food, there were billiard and pool tables for the members. Joseph Bergeron was the steward, an experienced restaurateur who offered members Saturday business lunches of lamb chops for fifty cents and evening meals of planked whitefish.

To the south at Iron Mountain is the Chippewa Club, housed in the former residence of the Chapin Mining Company manager, built in 1898. It was the idea of F. Albee Flodin and Martin D. Thomas to provide a clubhouse for visiting businessmen. It opened on December 11, 1946, as a private club supported by membership. It continues and is known for its fine dining and classic cocktail bar.

In Ishpeming, the Mather Inn was built basically for Cleveland Cliffs Mining Company executives, mining managers and businessmen, who were

Eve Arden and *Anatomy of a Murder* actors at the Mather Inn. *Superior View.*

joined by other mine officials and visitors. It opened in January 1932 with its grand Georgian Room and eventually, after Prohibition, a unique, cozy bar. Elaborate meals and celebrations were held, with formal wear required. In March–April 1959, it was home to the actors and actresses during the filming of *Anatomy of a Murder.* They enjoyed splendid meals in the dining room and refreshments. As the years passed and iron mining declined, so did the Mather Inn.

Less elegant were the clubs organized for workers. The Bay de Noquet Lumber Company (1881–1951) operated in the company town Nahma on the shores of Lake Michigan. It developed a series of clubhouses for its workers, the last one opening in 1949. South of Marquette, the Cleveland Cliffs Iron Company created the model town of Gwinn in 1910 and included a clubhouse, while the Northern Saw Mill Company developed the town of Sagola, north of Iron Mountain, and the Sagola Club House opened in May 1921. All of these clubhouses were recreation centers and offered light luncheons, including soda fountains, and hosted community gatherings.

SUPPER CLUB

The supper club is an American dining establishment concentrated in the Upper Midwest. It developed in the 1930s as an offshoot of the roadhouse of the Prohibition era and the private dining club. The supper club was seen as a "destination" with a casual and relaxed atmosphere but also a high-class image. The evening began with "expertly prepared cocktails," followed by dinner of American cuisine: prime rib, steaks, chicken, fish and fish fry. However, many of them added Italian food to internationalize the menu. The evening ended with dancing and entertainment.

The Dells Supper Club in Escanaba opened on April 5, 1933, to membership only but dropped this restriction and became widely known for its friendly, comfortable atmosphere. In 1936, it added a cocktail lounge. It remains the oldest supper club in the UP. The Northwoods Supper Club opened in Marquette at the same time, and four years later, the Three Mile Supper Club three miles west of Manistique emerged from Nick's Bar. At Spread Eagle, Wisconsin, three miles north of Iron Mountain, James and Rudy Manci opened the Riverside Club in 1937. At one time, it was the largest supper club north of Milwaukee. People throughout the Upper Peninsula took to the supper club concept, and it quickly spread across the region.

In their heyday, the clubs promoted banquet rooms that attracted community organizations for meetings, spring dances, high school events, entertainment and public lectures. Some offered "natural entertainment"; as you dined, you could watch wildlife, especially deer, pass in front of your dining window or you could enjoy a lake view or a colorful flower garden. The entertainment ranged from dancing to Ivan Kobasic's orchestra or Wimpy Smith to enjoying an Elvis impersonator or entertainment by a variety of singers and pianists at the keyboards.

The supper club was popular into the 1980s. Then dining attitudes changed, and many of the early clubs closed. Others, like the Dells, continue in operation but in a modified form.

THE SALAD BAR

An important restaurant feature in the Midwest and the Upper Peninsula was the salad bar. Complementing the supper club, it had its origins in Plover, Wisconsin, in 1950. Since it demanded a special refrigerated serving area, it took a while to enter the Upper Peninsula. However, in the UP, the concept of buffet dining goes back to Swedish immigrants and the smorgasbord. Thus, it was a relatively simple matter for Yoopers to take to the salad bar. By 1957, the Ojibway Hotel in the Soo had a salad bar. As the 1960s unfolded, it became part of the restaurant scene, and a restaurant without a salad bar was a rarity. As time passed, the salad bar became more of a smorgasbord by allowing you to make your own salad plus offering a hot plate with soups, meats, fish and vegetables, breads and desserts. You could order from the menu or serve yourself. Some restaurants, like the Northwoods Supper Club in Marquette, were known for their elaborate salad bars, and it was an event to go to dinner there. The heyday of the salad bar in the UP was from the 1970s into the 1990s, and today, it is no longer a major restaurant attraction. However, the Big Boy restaurants are one of the few to offer salad bar service.

FISH FRY

Naturally, those living in the Upper Peninsula did not have a problem getting fresh fish. One of the outcomes was the development of the Friday fish fry, which was quickly picked up by the general population. The first ads for a fish fry show up in the 1930s. In these early years, Prohibition had closed saloons, and owners turned to pool halls and soda fountains. They found that they could increase their revenue by serving fish, which was readily available and inexpensive. The other influence was the fact that the Catholics in the UP had to eat fish on Fridays and during Lent. The fish fry was born.

The first fish fries were offered by service clubs like the Elks in Sault Ste. Marie, which advertised heavily, but only to its members and friends. Later, the idea spread, and restaurants began serving fish fries. The plate consisted of local fish: whitefish, lake trout or perch and, in recent years, cod from the Atlantic. It was fried, deep fried or today grilled and served with first a salad and today coleslaw and a side of French fries. Usually, the meal is topped off with a beer.

The location of the fish fry was unlimited in the 1950s through 1970s. All the hotels in Escanaba offered fish fries. However, the House of Ludington served English fish and chips or fried perch dinners in the King George III Room, where you dined in elegance and finished the dinner with dancing to the Sparkling Emerald Trio. Supper clubs had fish fries. The exclusive Escanaba Country Club, open to members and guests, had a fish fry—

walleye, perch, whitefish and shrimp, including a salad bar. You could join a fish fry in Andy's Bar in Bark River, A&W root beer stands or Potvin's Tavern in Schaeffer, with some advertised as "the best in town."

Today, the fish fry continues to be an important ingredient in the culinary culture of the Upper Peninsula. The tradition that it is only offered on Fridays continues. Restaurants and service and veterans' clubs are filled with patrons seeking time to enjoy a traditional UP meal and socialize with friends and neighbors over their favorite beverage.

DRIVE-IN

Given the location of the Upper Peninsula in the far north, the idea of a drive-in is at times hard to comprehend. However, since the first drive-in opened in 1921 in Dallas, Texas, this type of restaurant found its way north. The drive-in restaurant developed beginning in the late 1940s with the opening of Clyde's in Sault Ste. Marie. This was followed by other Clyde's openings in Manistique and St. Ignace. Then across the UP, drive-in restaurants found their way, led by A&W. Some of the A&Ws went beyond curb service and offered full sit-down dining with roast turkey and the trimmings and fish fries. During the heyday—the 1950s through the 1970s—every town had its local drive-in, many of them fondly remembered like Big Al's and Hamburger Heaven in Marquette. Today, two A&Ws in Menominee and Iron Mountain remain open.

The Clyde's mini-chain remains open and has become the iconic drive-in restaurant in northern Michigan. Over the years, it has focused on healthy dining by serving bison burgers and salads. It is best known for its juicy "Big C": a three-quarter-pound of hamburger served on a bun the size of a pie tin along with crispy French fries—a meal for four. During 2020, the roller skates of the carhops were temporarily switched out for masks. Clyde's has reached icon status in Michigan. In Sault Ste. Marie, George and Gypsie Barbado opened West Pier Drive-In, and fifty years later, it is still serving the public. The fourth drive-in still operating is the Baraga Drive-In in the town of the same name. Big Al's famed hammy sammy and other delights are now found on the menu of Iron Bay Restaurant in Marquette.

Tourism promoter Mark Sabuco in 1954 opened a unique drive-in as part of his Indian village in Escanaba on major highways U.S. 41 and U.S. 2. A few years later, he opened another drive-in with a Paul Bunyan theme called

Clyde's Drive-In. *Author.*

Carhops dressed in a variety of costumes to highlight the service at Bud's Park 'n Eat, Munising. *Superior View.*

Babe & Bunyan Drive-In. It served the Paul Bunyan sandwich, "a meal in itself," and the Blue Oxburger. Others advertised, "Come as you are and eat in your car."

The drive-in has been replaced by the drive-through chains—Hardee's, McDonald's, Wendy's, DQ, Taco Bell, KFC—which have become even more popular with the Covid-19 pandemic of 2020–22. Long lines of autos filled the parking lots at mealtimes in all of these restaurants, as people sought to avoid crowded sit-down dining. This type of service continues to be popular.

RUSTIC RESTAURANTS

A unique characteristic of the Upper Peninsula is the woodland restaurant, which brings wilderness dining into the present. These eateries were started with the development of good highways beginning in the 1930s as places where people could escape the hectic present. Unfortunately, many of these outstanding culinary destinations have closed with changing travel preferences.

Located south of Munising and difficult to find was the Camel Riders Inn, an iconic and well-known resort and restaurant, which permanently closed in 2021, a victim of the coronavirus. It was established in the late 1940s as a place where people could enjoy the woods and a basic meal—steak, shrimp and lobster—and a beverage overlooking a beautiful lake setting far from the madding crowd. Also located in Alger County on Grand Island was the Williams Hotel, which the Cleveland Cliffs Iron Company opened to tourists in the 1930s. It was a bit of an experience, as guests took a ferry to the restaurant and then enjoyed a meal in the solitude of the forest.

The premier UP resort was Blaney Park Resort, located south of Germfask on M-77 near the U.S. 2 junction. It opened in 1928 on former cut-over timber land. It became a destination for family vacationers. Its rustic Knotty Pine Dining Room and cocktail lounge served extravagant lunch smorgasbords, and on Saturday evenings, tourists and locals went there to dine and stayed for entertainment featuring dance bands and "Saturday Night Skits" put on by the college student staff. As Americans changed vacation styles, the resort and its fine dining in the middle of the woods came to an end in 1967.

Fortunately, this dining experience has survived to be enjoyed year round. The region is known for its heavy snowfalls and as a result attracts snowmobilers from across the Midwest; many restaurants cater to these winter vacationers. The Buckhorn Resort, located fifteen minutes south of Munising, was established in 1933 as a general store and has grown into a rustic food destination with its bar and one-hundred-seat restaurant. The Brownstone Inn, west of Munising on M-28, opened in the late 1940s and continues to serve the passing public, locals and snowmobilers on their trail routes. For a few short weeks beginning on November 15, numerous restaurants and bars feature special meals, dances and entertainment for hunters who have wandered from their legendary hunting camps.

At the tip of the Keweenaw Peninsula is Copper Harbor, the north end of U.S. 41 and the home of the Keweenaw Mountain Lodge, constructed in 1933 as part of the New Deal's Works Progress Administration that brought relief to struggling communities. Logs from the land were used to construct cabins and a lodge filled with rustic charm. The lodge offers beverages, fine dining, private dinners and wedding banquets that return the guest to the past. In a unique appeal, guests borrow grill kits for a barbecue at their cabin.

The most curious of these restaurants is the Tahquamenon Brew Pub, a full-service restaurant, which is rare for brewpubs, where you usually bring your own eats. At first it seems that the brewpub is on Tahquamenon Falls State Park property because you enter the state parking lot to get to it. Does the State of Michigan own a brewery? No. In a rare development, the original owner of the land, Jack Barrett, kept some acreage when he donated a large parcel to the state, and thus the brewery has the distinction of being surrounded by state property.

At the remote eastern end of the UP is Drummond Island, the largest freshwater island in the United States, home to two restaurants: the Northwood Restaurant and Bar and the Drummond Island Resort and Conference Center. The latter resort was established by Domino's Pizza founder Tom Monaghan and in 2016 took on new owners. Its Pins Bar and Grille serves American cuisine and pizza.

NONTRADITIONAL DINING

Over the centuries, a variety of ships—passenger vessels, cruise ships, Coast Guard vessels, light ships and bulk carriers—have plied the waters around the Upper Peninsula. They are rarely viewed as eating places.

Because early visitors wanted to travel around the Upper Peninsula, they had to rely on steamers or, as they were called, "floating palaces." Suddenly, the boat trip north became a culinary adventure. However, the earliest travelers were horrified by the food served aboard ship. The owners had not yet realized that competitive travel was to be combined with fine dining in the wilderness.

The New York physician Chandler Gilman, who considered himself a bit of a gourmet, traveled to the UP in the summer of 1835 aboard the sailing vessel *White Pigeon*. The cook aboard was a "French Negro" named Antoine who provided the travelers with "sour bread or mouldy biscuit, thick muddy coffee, bad black tea." A side of beef hanging over the stern provided "steaks" fried in salt pork and served with potatoes. Gilman was scandalized by the poor quality of food en route.

As people traveled to the Upper Peninsula beginning in the 1840s, every effort was made for them to have a fine dining experience even in the middle of the wilderness. It took several days to travel from Detroit to Mackinac and Sault Ste. Marie and then across Lake Superior or along Lake Michigan.

The *Winslow* docked in Marquette Harbor carried a staff of a steward, chef and waiters. *Superior View*.

The dining salon aboard the *Japan*. *Superior View*.

The short-haul *General Scott*, which plied the waters between Mackinac Island and Sault Ste. Marie, had an airy dining room on the top deck that allowed passengers to dine and enjoy the passing scenery.

Passengers dined in the sumptuous dining saloons of the steamers overseen by stewards who gained reputations for their attention to detail around the Great Lakes. Many of the early ships had African American and Irish immigrant chefs and waitstaffs. Steamers had to stop for fuel every eight to ten hours, and at these wood landings, farmers were able to sell their produce and ice to passing ships. In 1846, Philetus S. Church was settled at Church's Landing on Sugar Island in the St. Mary's River. When the ships landed for wood, he refreshed the passengers with raspberry jam and provided the ships with maple syrup, vegetables, ice and milk. In the center of the shoreline of Lake Superior lies Grand Island, which was another landing for steamboat wood. Here, Abraham Williams also developed a forty-acre farm beginning in 1841 and provided ships with potatoes, turnips, beets and cabbages. The latter landing was especially welcomed during stormy weather on the lake.

The concern for fine dining while en route to and around the Upper Peninsula continues to the present day. For instance, the menu for June 1927 aboard the *Eastern States* featured appetizers, baked Lake Huron whitefish Creole, soups and relishes, followed by a choice of roast young duck, giblet dressing and strawberry preserves; roast baby lamb with currant jelly;

The climate and soil of the UP produce cabbage and other crops that help meet the demand for locally produced food. *Superior View.*

breaded pork tenderloin with baked apple; or vegetable dinner with poached egg, followed by an array of desserts and a cheese and cracker platter. The Captain's Dinner aboard the popular SS *North American* in August 1950 opened with fresh shrimp cocktail or French onion soup with these choices for the main course: broiled fillet Great Lakes trout, maître d'hotel; charcoal broiled sirloin steak, mushroom sauce; vegetables and potatoes; and a variety of desserts. This tradition continues aboard cruise ships that visit UP waters believing that "the culinary experience aboard our ships is an intrinsic part of the overall voyage."

The bulk freighters known as "ore boats" have visited UP destinations since the 1850s. The cook and assistants and the steward have to be sure that the crew is well fed, trying not to get too fancy, but the goal is to keep the crew happy. Breakfast can consist of omelets and bacon; lunch can be turkey wraps and hamburgers; and dinner can be more elaborate. One meal in 2015 aboard the longest ship on the Great Lakes, the *MV Paul R. Tregurtha*, consisted of eighty fried perch fillets; seven marinated pork tenderloins seasoned with thyme and garlic; acorn squash coated in butter, pecans and brown sugar; baked potatoes; broccoli with cheese sauce; and pineapple upside-down cake. There are always plenty of snacks, cookies and cakes, much as would be found at home. Passengers can book passage on some of these ships and partake in shipboard dining.

LUMBER CAMPS

The lumber camps scattered throughout the UP in the late nineteenth century have their own culinary heritage. In the camps, the men worked during the winter, and their work was grueling, which required heavy caloric consumption. If a company had bad food, it could easily lose its work crew. The workday began with the cook or cookie (as the assistant was referred to) and teamsters up at 4:30 or 5:00 a.m. The men were breakfasted with pancakes with molasses, fried potatoes, fried salt pork in strips, prunes three times a day, cookies, doughnuts, cake squares and coffee with condensed milk and were in the woods by daybreak. Hot lunches were brought to the men in the woods and could consist of stew or hunks of meat, boiled rice and potatoes, pies and coffee. Supper came after 6:30 p.m. and consisted of soup, boiled beef and potatoes, beans, bread, cookies, doughnuts and more pie. The meals in the bunkhouse were taken in silence since conversation

Cookie with his family with a horn to call in the lumberjacks for dinner. *Superior View.*

The dining room of Diamond Camp No. 3. *Superior View.*

was frowned upon. Not all of the men were satisfied with the regular meals, and some had snacks. Three-hundred-pound, six-foot-three-inch Edward Morrow, a sleigh boss, had a favorite snack: a half-inch slice of salt pork between two slices of cake.

The meals were huge, as cooks were concerned about quality and quantity. In one week, a one-hundred-man camp consumed the following amounts of food: six barrels of flour, two and a half barrels of beef, two and a half barrels of salted pork, eight bushels of potatoes, three bushels of onions, one barrel of pickles, one barrel of sugar, fifty pounds of butter, forty pounds of lard, twenty-five pounds of tea and sixteen pounds of coffee. When possible, deer were hunted and fish were caught for the meals. The cook's larder also held prunes, dried fruit, sausage, spices and condiments. A good cook made a camp run smoothly; when the stomach was full, there was little trouble with drunken sprees. A camp cook was paid sixty to one hundred dollars a month, while a dining car cook received twenty to twenty-five dollars per month.

RESTAURANTS ON MACKINAC ISLAND

The epicenter of diverse and intriguing cuisine in the Upper Peninsula is Mackinac Island. Day visitors are pleased to find burgers, pizza and other fast-food delights, but this is not true for those who arrive for a several-day stay. As a result, a collection of fine restaurants with fantastic views and food has developed along with quaint small eateries. In the early days, food was available in the hotel you stayed at, but by the mid-twentieth century, more than quaint tea shops were to be found along Main Street. In recent years, the island has had dozens of restaurants that cater to all budgets and tastes. One of the hallmarks of food on the island is using Michigan foods. Thus, at this juncture, the culinary past and the present are joined. One heritage food that most visitors order during their stay on the island is fresh whitefish and lake trout. The Village Inn, one of two restaurants that operates year round, offers fried whitefish and chips, broiled fresh whitefish, Heart Smart whitefish, whitefish sandwich and Great Lakes whitefish chowder. Planked whitefish is an island favorite: fresh fillet surrounded with piped mashed potatoes and garnished with fresh vegetables, then baked on a maple board. During the summer season, the Village Inn serves as many as ninety to one hundred orders a day. The restaurants avoid staid carrots and broccoli for

The Grand Hotel, Mackinac Island. *Author.*

local asparagus, tender butternut squash, roasted red pepper and Parmesan-crusted tomatoes. Horn's Gaslight Bar, reputedly the recipient of either the first or one of the first liquor licenses in Michigan after Prohibition, takes on a Southwest and Mexican food theme; Patrick Sinclair's Irish Pub offers Irish-themed food, including potato boxty, shepherd's pie and Irish stew.

The capstone of the restaurants on the island is the Grand Hotel, which opened in 1887. Between 1991 and 2019, the executive chef was Austrian-trained Han Burtscher, who moved the menus into the twenty-first century. As he pointed out, in the past, 50 to 60 percent of the guests ordered prime rib or whitefish, and that dropped to 30 percent with the arrival of new cuisines. To maintain variety, he changed the menus every three days.

The executive chef oversees all of the Grand Hotel's restaurants: the Main Dining Room, the Jockey Club at the Grand Strand, Woods Restaurant, the Gate House, Sushi Grand and Fort Mackinac Tea Room. In the Main Dining Room, six hundred to eight hundred guests can be served during two sittings. However, the Woods serves two hundred guests, and as a result, the chef is able to focus on new recipes.

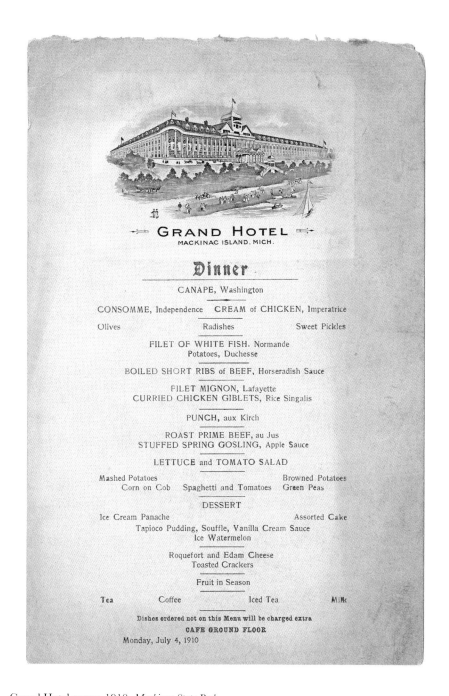

GRAND HOTEL
MACKINAC ISLAND, MICH.

Dinner

CANAPE, Washington

CONSOMME, Independence   CREAM of CHICKEN, Imperatrice

Olives   Radishes   Sweet Pickles

FILET OF WHITE FISH. Normande
Potatoes, Duchesse

BOILED SHORT RIBS of BEEF, Horseradish Sauce

FILET MIGNON, Lafayette
CURRIED CHICKEN GIBLETS, Rice Singalis

PUNCH, aux Kirch

ROAST PRIME BEEF, au Jus
STUFFED SPRING GOSLING, Apple Sauce

LETTUCE and TOMATO SALAD

Mashed Potatoes   Browned Potatoes
Corn on Cob   Spaghetti and Tomatoes   Green Peas

DESSERT

Ice Cream Panache   Assorted Cake
Tapioco Pudding, Souffle, Vanilla Cream Sauce
Ice Watermelon

Roquefort and Edam Cheese
Toasted Crackers

Fruit in Season

Tea   Coffee   Iced Tea   Milk

Dishes ordered not on this Menu will be charged extra
CAFE GROUND FLOOR
Monday, July 4, 1910

Grand Hotel menu, 1910. *Mackinac State Park.*

The Main Dining Room at the Grand Hotel. *Superior View.*

The buffet breakfast is unmatched in its variety of items, including all kinds of eggs and omelets and biscuits with ham. The Grand luncheon buffet is a once-in-a-lifetime experience, and for many, it is the reason for coming to Mackinac Island. In the Main Dining Room, the old standards—leg of lamb, prime rib, mixed grill and fish from Michigan waters—dominate the menu. The following provides a mere glimpse into the changing menus: appetizer of rabbit terrine; foie gras mousse, Michigan wild berry mustard and sourdough or buffalo tenderloin carpaccio with mustard sauce; chilled English pea soup or berry citrus and heirloom tomato salad; and for the entrée, maple-glazed Michigan lake trout, fennel-crusted lamb chops and whitefish terrine with an edible orchid.

The sommelier oversees 180 wines and 60 more on the captain's list of "limited availability"; 28 wines are served from the bottle. Not to be outdone, the variety of spirits available rises to the occasion, from fine whiskeys to Louis XIII brandy for those inclined.

As a result, the hotel has the largest kitchen in the world and employs a staff of two hundred. Two bakers, beginning at 10:00 p.m., prepare approximately four thousand croissants and half as many Danish for breakfast. The bakery on a daily basis uses 75 pounds of sugar and 50 pounds of flour, baking in fifteen-foot ovens. In past seasons, 13,275 pounds of mound shrimp, 32,703 pounds of chickens and sixteen prime ribs weighing 600 pounds have been served. In one season, the bakers, making sixty thousand of their famous pecan balls, used 819 pounds of pecans and 5,115 pounds of chocolate. As many as four thousand meals are served daily.

CHAPTER 7
Promotion and Preservation of Foodways

A s we reach the epilogue of this edible quest, it is important to recognize how individuals and organizations preserve and promote Upper Peninsula foodways beyond the confines above the Bridge and into the culinary world at large. They are numerous and varied in their approaches.

Chase S. Osborn (1860–1949) was a multifaceted Yooper who went from game warden to governor of Michigan (1911–13) by way of newspaper reporter and explorer. His experiences with food come forth in *Northwoods Sketches*, where he provides an appreciation and understanding of food on the borders of the frontier and also shows how you can survive in the deep woods. He concluded, "Ideally in order to enjoy fish to the utmost one should live close to water, go fishing one hour before the meal."

In 1919, Ernest M. Hemingway (1899–1961) came to the UP with friends to fish at Seney on the Fox River. The result was his famed short story "Big Two Hearted River." In it, his character Nick Adams provides us with north woods meals: buckwheat cakes and apple butter for breakfast, onion sandwich for lunch and a blend of canned pork and beans and spaghetti, topped off with catsup and bread, for dinner, with canned apricots for dessert. In 1920, Hemingway wrote for the *Toronto Star*, focusing on rumrunning "Canuck whiskey" into the United States across Lake Superior.

John Voelker (1903–1991) of Ishpeming, state supreme court justice and author, is best known for *Anatomy of a Murder*. On the pages of his numerous novels and short stories, he brought the reader from the woods and fishing streams into the world of food created by immigrants, which included Finnish celebrations, pasties, polenta, "old mulligan stew, consisting of venison, rabbit, partridge, beaver and whatever was available." As an avid fisherman, he provides us with his recipe for fried fish: "But by far the best time to enjoy your trout is beside the waters where they are caught. Take a fry pan along and some bacon or shortening, and a little cornmeal and salt, and have yourself a feast fit for a king—or an ulcerated millionaire." He takes us into the depths of "dining in the woods."

The last of these authors is self-described gourmand and author Jim Harrison (1937–2016), who spent summers at his getaway home in Grand Marais. In his two novels centered on the UP—*True North* and *Returning to Earth*—he uses his food expertise to intertwine the novels with local food and drink. His main character, David Burkett, "loved Mrs. Plunkett because she was daffy and cooked us Italian food which was a delicious and startling contrast to the anemic WASP food my mother fixed." Abbreviated fish recipes appear: roasting fish with dry vermouth, butter and lemon or brook trout "fried with some bacon grease mixed with butter," enjoyed with bread and topped off with blueberry cobbler. On Harrison's pages appear venison mincemeat pie and a bachelor's "culinary victory": "chopped onion and a jar of baked beans over the chops in a frying pan." Not to be forgotten is both dago red and vintage wines along with schnapps, brandy and six-packs of beer.

Fundraising cookbooks developed by local church and community groups are sources of typical local recipes, but despite a move to Americanize the immigrant through the promotion of American foods, some immigrant recipes have survived. The most unique of these books is that developed by Mina Valli titled *Keittokirjä/Cookbook* and written for Finnish domestic servants who had to prepare meals in American homes. Her goal was to improve the position and salary of the servant, "as well as the empathy of the family in the household." It was so popular that it went through three revised editions by 1923. Today, the few copies of this bilingual cookbook that survive are a treasure-trove of authentic UP Finnish recipes in the early twentieth century..

Since 1899, Michigan State University has maintained the UP Research and Extension Center in Chatham. It exists to conduct "experiments pertaining to agriculture and horticulture…beneficial to the agriculture interests of the Upper Peninsula." In 2012, MSU Center for Regional Foods Systems was established to advance regionally rooted food systems through applied research, education and outreach.

The food revolution began in the 1970s, and in the late twentieth century, Yoopers became concerned about healthy diets based on locally grown foods and improved nutrition. As a result, small farms developed growing seasonal foods, which allowed people to know the origins of their foods. By the twenty-first century, the UP had over one hundred local farms, and farmers' markets are found in every community in the UP. Apiaries have developed along with sugar bushes, which sell their products in groceries around the Peninsula. Since the 1850s, cattle ranches have operated in the UP. In 1988, the Circle K Buffalo Farm opened in Rudyard, followed by the Beaver Grove Bison Farm south of Marquette opening around 2009. Duck eggs are available, as are indoor-grown mushrooms. The Marquette Food Co-op and the Keweenaw Co-op in Hancock are two of a number in the UP whose goal "is to provide the community with organically grown fruit and vegetables and to sell products that follow healthy patterns of production."

There has been a return to Native American origins of food. Beginning in 2010, Dr. Martin Reinhardt of the Center for Native American Studies at Northern Michigan University directed the Decolonizing Diet Project, which uses Anishinaabe ethnobotany to study the relationship between humans and native foods. MSU works with the Native American Western UP Food System Collaborative, organized in 2018, a grassroots community effort to promote "the unique gifts of the land." The Keweenaw Bay Ojibwa Community College developed the *Ojibwa Recipe Book*.

A number of schools have developed culinary arts programs that are popular with students. These are found at Lake Superior State University and in Northern Michigan University's Hospitality Tourism Management program. The Cedarville Culinary School at Hessel is a private institution. At NMU, the restaurant Chez Nous is open during the school year, and the Cedarville facility is only open in the summer, as the students train in the winter.

Over the decades, the UP has been home to many outstanding chefs. Two of them—Harold "Pat" Hayes and Nathan D. Mileski—are examples of chefs from different eras: the mid-twentieth century and the early twenty-first century.

As we have seen, the House of Ludington in Escanaba has had a long history of fine dining, and onto the scene came the legendary hotelier and chef Pat Hayes (1897–1969). Born in South Boston, he trained in food service in Chicago. He arrived in the UP, liked what he saw and decided to stay and bought the House of Ludington in 1939. He developed as a master chef and spent the next thirty years turning the hotel's dining room into the most renowned in the UP. He installed an ultra-modern electric kitchen. The King George III (yes, named after the king who lost the American Revolution) Room was graced with Waterford crystal, Irish linens, gold punch bowls and silver venison dishes. He warned the dishwashers to be careful with dishes valued at sixteen dollars each.

The appointments matched the food that he cooked for all of his guests, some of whom traveled hundreds of miles to dine with him. The restaurant was famed for its service. In Hayes's kitchen, he used only fresh ingredients—meat, fish fowl, fruit. As he said, "I can prepare and serve anything the Waldorf Astoria does," and often he did. He could readily prepare "baked squab in cantaloupe and stuffed with brandied peaches served under glass" or a fine steak, but he only prepared well-done steaks with poorer cuts of meat, saying, "That's no way to treat fine meat." For a hunters' dinner one year, he served flaming pheasant on a sword. Hayes was known for his elaborate themed banquets that he frequently presented in the 1950s.

House
Of
Ludington

Presents
A Night in Paris

Le Buffet Elegant
Hors D'Oeuvres—Variety of Appetizers
Vichyssoise—French Potato-Leek Soup
Croissants—French Crescents
Brioche—French Rolls
Coquilles Saint-Jacques—Baked Scallops
Quenelles Sauce Royale—Pike Quenelles
Grenouille de Gourmet—Frog Legs
Homard Droumant—Fresh Lobster Thermidor
Crab Louie—Crabmeat
Sole Marguery—Filet of Sole
Tourte Lorraine—Pork and Veal Pie
Fillet Joseph—Broiled Beef Tenderloin with Mushroom and Wine Sauce
Poulet de Brisse au Vin ala Creme—Sauteed Chicken in Wine and Cream
Ris de Veau ala Creme—Creamed Sweet Breads
Fluetters Alsacienne—Potato Puffs

Petit Pois ala Francais—French Peas with Onions-Herbs
Asperges ala Normande—Asparagus with Normandy Sauce
Tomato Farcie—Stuffed Tomato
Salade Margot—Banana-Celery-Curry and Almond Oil
Macédoine de Fruit—Assorted Fresh Fruits
Salade Cauchoise—Potato Salad
Salade de Laitues—Lettuce Salad-Bibb-Romaine-Escarole
Cammembert ala Bar le Duc—Imported Camembert Cheese and Currant
Jelly
Pâtisseries ala Francaise—Assorted French Pastries including
Baba au rhum—Rum Cake
Crepes Suzette— French Pancakes served with
Orange and Curacao Sauce Flambe (Flaming)

Over the years, Hayes offered meticulous service to Michigan governors Soapy Williams and George Romney; Prince Bertil of Sweden; several executives from Marshall Fields of Chicago; the Blocks of Inland Steel; Jimmy Hoffa, president of the Teamsters' Union; syndicated columnist Ann Landers; and many others. His attention to detail did not end with the rich and powerful but extended to the regular diners who entered his realm. It was only natural that his reputation for fine dining extended across the Midwest.

Onto the scene at the inception of the twenty-first century came Nathan D. Mileski, a Marquette native who exemplifies the blending of traditional foods and cooking of the Upper Peninsula with modern cuisine. He comes from a diverse ethnic background—Polish, German, Irish, southern American—and grew up cooking with wild vegetables (fiddlehead ferns, morels, ramps) and game (deer, elk, moose, rabbit). This gave him a special feel for cooking, and he has said, "My food comes out much differently because I have had experience with it." He trained at the renowned Culinary Institute of America at Hyde Park, New York. In 2009, he became a certified executive chef, having been preceded by David Sonderschafer, the first such chef in the UP.

After working at a number of restaurants in the UP, Mileski became director of food services at Northern Michigan University, his alma mater, where he trained many students. He first competed in the National Association of College and University Food Services culinary competition in 2009, winning the Midwest regional and then the nationals. His award-winning creation was trout schnitzel: a thin slice of veal coated in breadcrumbs and fried, served with spätzle and möhrengemüse carrots. Over the years, he and his team of students won gold, silver and bronze awards and put the UP on the culinary map. Despite his training and awards, his food philosophy remains "cooking great, simple food," and he concludes, "There is nothing better than a perfectly roasted chicken." In 2021, he opened the Yoop Coop in Marquette, serving hand-breaded or grilled tenders with twenty-three sauces for dunking along with mac-n-cheese, sandwiches and salads on the menu.

FOOD FESTIVALS

Over the years, a number of food-related festivals have developed throughout the Upper Peninsula based on foods produced in the area. By the 1870s, strawberry and ice cream festivals were commonly celebrated by various churches as fundraisers. In 1871, the Knights Templar of Escanaba held a "Grand Strawberry & Ice Cream Festival" in their hall as part of the July 4 celebration. Other festivals continued into the early twentieth century. County potato harvesting ended in October with the UP festival that rotated from community to community, where the best potatoes from across the UP were judged. The dream of a young girl was to be voted potato queen. In the 1930s, elaborate and nationally celebrated smelt jamborees were held in Menominee and Escanaba, and tons of the small silvery fish collected by local residents were shipped around the Midwest. Other towns had smaller festivals as well. At the same time, the city of Manistique in the heart of blueberry country developed the National Blueberry Festival in 1939. These festivals lasted into the 1950s. The Upper Peninsula State Fair, which was organized in 1928, is held in Escanaba and provides awards for the best food products and processed foods, which encourages better crops. This is the only state fair in Michigan.

Other less elaborate food festivals developed across the UP. The Copper Country Strawberry Festival at Chassell began in 1949 and continues. The Munising Moose Lodge has been holding a fish derby since 1984. The Marquette Blueberry Festival began in 2001 and provides blueberry-related foods like pizza, sausage and beer. The latter became so popular that it is served throughout the summer by some brewpubs. The Wild Blueberry Festival is held in Paradise. In the heart of the Keweenaw Peninsula since 1999, the Thimbleberry Jam Fest has been celebrated at Mohawk, north of Calumet. In the latter town since 2004, the annual Pasty Fest is held.

Above: Smelting from the interstate bridge, Menominee, Michigan. *Superior View.*

Left: King Fish Long was crowned King of Semtonia. *Superior View.*

Across the Peninsula, the annual Mackinac Island Fudge Festival has been held since 2019. In June of that year, the Cudighi Cook-Off and Festival was inaugurated in Ishpeming. Fifteen restaurants participated, and judges tested the sauce, bread, meat and overall presentation in selecting a winner. The first Cudighi World Champion was the Teal Lake Pizzeria.

A Seafood Festival is held in Houghton, and the UP Fall Beer Festival held in September in Marquette attracts sixty craft brewers presenting four hundred different labels. In Ishpeming, the St. Rocco and St. Anthony Society has held an annual festival since 1899. Today, the festa is held in August and offers Italian pasta, pizza and desserts and is the last of such Italian food festas in the UP. All of these festivals were interrupted in 2020–22 because of the Covid-19 pandemic, but they have been revived.

Over the years, the foods of the Upper Peninsula have been promoted first by newspapers and then by television programs. The *Detroit Free Press* and other downstate newspapers provided stories about travel to the Upper Peninsula and then gave directions to foods, including pasties, Mackinac fudge, Trenary toast and whitefish. Even during the midst of the coronavirus pandemic in 2020, the paper, along with *USA Today*, presented a tour of the UP for the homebound and discussed Clyde's Drive-In at St. Ignace, Jean Kay's Pasties and Subs in Marquette, Peterson's Fish Market in Hancock, Fitzgerald's Hotel and Restaurant in Eagle River and Rock Skipper's Fish & Chips in Copper Harbor. For those who cannot travel to the UP but want the foods, there are ads for Michigan Maple Farms and Murdick's Fudge on Mackinac Island,

The foods of the UP have drawn Andrew Zimmern with his TV show *Bizarre Foods, Delicious Destinations* to the area, where he visited restaurants with iconic foods such as the pasty, whitefish and cudighi. *Lost in Michigan*, a state program, has also visited the area and focused on food.

The culinary journey has gone from Native American foods to a creolization of foods and the introduction of new foods. Even within this relatively isolated region of the country, the food story can be told along with the development of new and unique of restaurants, brewpubs and distilleries—a new world of food on the northern border.

APPENDIX

Recipes from the Upper Peninsula

Over the years, a number of food and beverage recipes have surfaced that are traditional to the UP. They are presented here for your enjoyment and to provide you with a taste of this unique region that brings the region alive.

Wild Rice Breakfast
A dish that combines all of the elements of Native American foods.
—Shannon Dikkema, Marquette

1 cup wild rice
Blueberries to taste
Maple syrup to taste

Cook the wild rice in water until the kernels pop open and then place it in a bowl. Add the berries and syrup and enjoy.

Venison Jerky

Dried meat to mix with corn or wild rice was an important part
of the Anishinaabe diet.

—Martin Reinhardt, originally from Baweting/Sault Ste. Marie

2 pounds venison
Handful of salt
Handful of maple sugar

Cut about 2 to 2½ pounds of venison (cut with the grain so the meat does not fall apart when dry) about ¼ inch thick so that all the pieces are roughly the same thickness; length does not matter. Using a gallon bowl, fill the bottom with sea salt and maple sugar. Fill halfway with water. Place strips in the bucket and sprinkle more sea salt and maple sugar over meat and top it off with water. Mix the meat and let it sit overnight in the refrigerator. Place on smoker grill and let strips brown and dry until they reach a jerky consistency. Remove and store in a dry, airtight container.

Strawberry and Watermelon Soup

Han Burtscher, former chef of the Grand Hotel, provided
this popular recipe in 2013.

2 cups seedless watermelon
2 cups cleaned strawberries
⅓ cup Midori (melon-flavored liqueur)
1 whole vanilla bean
½ cup yogurt
½ cup sour cream
¼ cup powdered sugar
3 tablespoons honey
1 tablespoon cinnamon

First, cut the rind of 1 watermelon and the stems and leaves off the strawberries. Dice the meat from the fruit into cubes, place them into a large bowl and pour the Midori over the top. While the Midori is soaking into the fruit, slice the vanilla bean lengthwise and, with a spoon, remove the bean pulp and discard the outer shell.

Place the fruit, bean pulp and remaining ingredients into a large blender and blend on high until all the ingredients are mixed and there is a smooth consistency. Pour this mixture into a bowl and chill until you are ready to serve.

Tourtière/Pork Pie

This traditional food from Québec, a favorite with French Canadians, is prepared at Christmastime.
—Shannon Dikkema, Marquette

2 tablespoons vegetable oil
1 pound ground pork
1 pound ground veal
1 pound ground beef
3 cloves garlic, minced
3 onions, minced
Bay leaf, whole
¼ teaspoon cinnamon
¼ teaspoon ground cloves
2 tablespoons parsley flakes
1 tablespoon dry celery leaves
½ teaspoon celery seeds
2 cups beef broth
2 ounces brandy
½ cup fresh breadcrumbs
2 teaspoons salt
1 teaspoon pepper
Flaky pastry for 3 double-crust 9-inch pies
1 large egg, beaten

Heat oil in a large, heavy frying pan and fry the meat with the garlic, onions and spices; then add the broth, cover and simmer for 20 minutes. Add brandy, breadcrumbs and salt and pepper and simmer a little longer. Line pans with pastry; fill the pasty with the mixture. Cover pastry, cutting slits for the steam to escape, and brush with egg wash. Bake at 425 degrees for 30 minutes.

Rutabaga Casserole (*Lanttuaatikko*)
This is a traditional dish at Finnish Little Christmas
and was served with a meat dish.
—Esko Alasimi, Marquette

2 medium rutabagas, peeled and diced (about 6 cups)
¼ cup fine dry breadcrumbs
¼ cup cream
½ teaspoon nutmeg
1 teaspoon salt
2 eggs, beaten
3 tablespoons butter

Cook the rutabagas until soft (about 20 minutes) in salted water to cover. Drain and mash. Soak the breadcrumbs in the cream and stir in the nutmeg, salt and beaten eggs. Combine with mashed rutabaga. Turn into a buttered 2½-quart casserole, dot the top with butter and bake in a moderate oven (350 degrees) for 1 hour or until lightly browned on top. Serves 6 to 8.

Swedish Rye Bread (*Limpa*)
This traditional bread was brought to the UP by Swedish immigrants.
Some women made rye bread for every meal, and their homes were
filled with the aroma of bread.

3 cups medium rye flour
½ cup dark molasses
¼ cup shortening
1 tablespoon salt
1 package dry yeast
5 cups flour

Combine the first four ingredients in a bowl. Stir in yeast and flour to make a stiff dough. Knead on floured surface for 10 minutes. Place in greased bowl, cover and let rise in a warm place until doubled (about

2 hours). Punch down. Let rise for 30 minutes. Shape into 3 balls, cover and let rise for 10 minutes. Shape into round or long loaves. Place in greased pan. Cover and let rise until very light, 1 to 1¼ hours. Bake at 375 degrees for 30 to 35 minutes.

Pasty
This 1911 recipe comes from Ethel Morcom Rule
and is a very traditional pasty recipe.

3 cups flour
1 cup suet, ground fine
½ cup lard
1 teaspoon salt
6–7 tablespoons cold water
1 pound diced or cubed good-quality beef
½ pound diced or cubed good-quality pork
Ample potatoes, onions and rutabagas, finely cubed or diced
A few knobs of butter, pepper, parsley and a bit of salt

Combine the first five ingredients—flour, suet, lard, salt and cold water—and mix. Then take the prepared meat and vegetables, mix them and place in the middle of a circle of dough. Fold dough and crimp. Bake at 400 degrees for 1 hour (wood stove temperature.)

Bagna Cauda
Meaning literally "hot bath," this is a traditional appetizer
from Piedmont, Italy.
—Letizia Pitrone, Bessemer, Michigan

1 2-ounce can anchovies
1 teaspoon garlic, finely chopped (more or less to taste)
¼ tablespoon butter
¼ cup peanut or olive oil
1 cup heavy cream

Combine anchovies, garlic, butter and oil in a heavy-bottom saucepan. Simmer very slowly for half an hour, stirring constantly. Anchovies will disintegrate. Slowly add cream and then bring to a simmer, stirring constantly (about 5 minutes).

Serve warm in a bowl or in a fondue pot in which to dip cold vegetables—red and green peppers, celery stalks cut into strips, savoy cabbage or romaine lettuce broken into separate leaves or cauliflower separated into florets. Serves 6 to 8.

Torchetti
Cookies from Piedmont were popular with Italians,
especially at Christmastime.
—Connie Pricco, Bessemer, Michigan

1 pound butter
5 cups flour
2 eggs
1 tablespoon vanilla
3 tablespoons sugar
2 packages yeast
½ cup milk

Soften the butter at room temperature and mix thoroughly with flour. Mix eggs, vanilla and sugar together. Dissolve yeast into tepid milk and add beaten egg mixture. Mix thoroughly with the flour and butter mixture and mold into a ball. Cover with a cloth and let rise for 1½ hours at room temperature. Pinch a small piece of dough and roll out to the size of a small finger (½ inch diameter) and approximately 8 inches long and bend to the shape of a torchetti (circle heart). Dip lightly into sugar and bake on ungreased cookie sheet in 350-degree oven for 12 to 14 minutes or until golden.

Ludington Chocolate Strata Pie

This recipe is from the House of Ludington and became popular
in many areas of the UP.
—Karen Lindquist, Escanaba

Pie Shell Crust
1 cup all-purpose flour
½ teaspoon salt
½ cup shortening
2–4 tablespoons cold water

Combine ingredients to prepare a one-crust pie shell. Prick shell with fork and bake at 450 degrees for 10 to 12 minutes, or until golden brown.

Filling: First Layer
½ teaspoon vinegar
¼ teaspoon salt
¼ teaspoon cinnamon (if desired)
2 egg whites
½ cup sugar

Combine the vinegar, salt and cinnamon with the egg whites. Beat the mixture until soft mounds form and then add ½ cup sugar gradually until meringue stands in stiff, glossy peaks. Spread on the bottom and sides of the baked pie shell. Bake at 325 degrees for 15 to 18 minutes, or until slightly browned.

Chocolate Whipped Cream Filling: Second Layer
2 slightly beaten egg yolks
¼ cup water
1 cup semisweet chocolate pieces, melted

Combine ingredients and spread about 3 tablespoons over the cooled meringue. Chill remainder.

Final Layer
¼ cup sugar
¼ teaspoon cinnamon
1 cup whipping cream

Beat ingredients until thick. Combine with the remaining whipped cream and chocolate mixture. Spread over whipped cream in the pie shell. Chill at least 4 hours.

Anaconda

In the first half of the twentieth century, the Beach Inn was a popular resort hotel on the shore of Munising Bay. The Anaconda is probably the most iconic beverage created in the UP and is presented here for your enjoyment. Any liquor can be used, but the white liquors allow the maple flavor to stand out.

1–2 ounces gin or vodka
1 ounce maple syrup
Lemon juice, to taste

Fill a cocktail shaker with ice and pour in gin or vodka. Add maple syrup and lemon juice. The juice cuts the sweetness and viscosity of the heavier syrup. Shake well until mixed and cold. Pour into a chilled cocktail glass.

StumpKnockers

This drink was a perennial favorite at the cocktail lounge at the Blaney Park Resort during the 1940s and 1950s.

1 ounce brandy
1 ounce rum
1 ounce triple sec
½ ounce lemon juice
Dash of bitters

Mix in a cocktail shaker with ice and serve in any glass available.

Peter White Punch

This punch was "discovered" by pioneer Peter White and first served at the fiftieth anniversary celebration of the opening of the Soo Canal in 1905. It is a strong beverage and expensive to make, and it must be consumed with caution.

1 quart Jamaica rum
1 quart Santa Cruz rum
1 bottle Curaçao
1 bottle Chartreuse
1 bottle Maraschino
1 quart English breakfast tea
5 pounds white sugar
2 bottles Champagne
½ dozen lemons
½ dozen oranges

Set a piece of ice 8 inches square in the middle of the punch bowl. Combine first five ingredients. One hour before serving the punch, put in 1 quart of strong cold English breakfast tea and 5 pounds of white sugar. One-half hour before serving, put in 2 bottles of good Champagne. At the same time, thinly slice one-half dozen lemons (include the skins of the lemons) and one-half dozen oranges. You can also use two bottles of Apollinaris or any mineral water with the Champagne.

Bibliography

Armour, David A., and Keith R. Widder. *At the Crossroads: Michilimackinac during the American Revolution.* Mackinac Island, MI: Mackinac Island State Park Commission, 1978.

Armstrong, Julian. *A Taste of Québec.* New York: Hippocrene Books, Inc., 2001.

Askin, John. *The John Askin Papers.* Edited by Milo M. Quaife. Detroit, MI: Detroit Library Commission, 1928 and 1931.

Blanchette, Jean-François. "The Role of Artifacts in the Study of Foodways in New France, 1720–1760: Two Case Studies Based on the Analysis of Ceramic Artifacts." PhD dissertation, Brown University, 1979.

Brown, Cecilia. "Blaney Park, the U.P.'s 'Premier Resort.'" *The Mining Journal*, February 22, 2018.

Carlson, Jeanna K. *Culinary Creolization: Subsistence and Cultural Interaction at Fort Michilimackinac, 1730–1761.* Archaeological Completion Report Series, No. 18. Mackinac Island, MI: Mackinac State Historic Parks, 2012.

Childs, Mrs. W.A. [Susan] "Reminiscences of 'Old Keweenaw.'" *Michigan Pioneer and Historical Collection* 30 (1906): 150–55.

Clark, Morton G. *French-American Cooking from New Orleans to Québec.* New York: Funk & Wagnalls, 1967.

Curto, Don, and Patricia J. Tikkanen. *Stirring It Up!* Edited by Erin Elliott and Pat Ryan O'Day. Marquette, MI: Thumbs Up Publishing, 2002.

Densmore, Frances. *Chippewa Customs.* Washington, D.C.: Smithsonian Institution, Bureau of American Ethnology. *Bulletin 86*, 1929; reprint, St. Paul: Minnesota Historical Society, 1979.

Did They Really Eat That?: A 19th Century Cookbook that Acquainted Immigrants with Northwoods Pioneer Fare. Lake Linden, MI: Keweenaw Press, 1992.

Dupras, Joyce Hill, et al. *The Joy of Finnish-American Cooking*. Gurnee, IL: Hääpänen/ Burkett, Inc., 2005.

Egan-Bruhy, Kathryn. "Floral Analysis: Fort Drummond (20CH50), an Early Nineteenth Century British Fort, Drummond Island, Michigan." Museum Archaeology Program, State Historical Society of Wisconsin, circa 2009.

Eustice, Sally. *History from the Hearth: A Colonial Michilimackinac Cookbook*. Mackinac Island, MI: Mackinac Island State Park Commission, 1997.

Evans, Lynn L.M. *House D of the Southeast Row House: Excavations at Fort Michilimackinac, 1989–1997*. Archaeological Completion Series, Number 17. Mackinac Island, MI: Mackinac State Historic Parks, 2001.

Forester, John H. "Early Settlement of the Copper Regions of Lake Superior." *Michigan Pioneer and Historical Collection* 7 (1886): 181–93.

Friggens, Thomas G. *"Peas Upon a Trencher": A Study of Diet at Fort Wilkins*. Copper Harbor, MI: Fort Wilkins Natural History Association, 1985.

Frimodig, David "Mac." "With Mayt, Turmit, and Tatey." *Michigan Natural Resources Magazine*, January–February 1971, 22.

Gagnon, John. *Hard Maple, Hard Work*. Marquette: Northern Michigan University Press, 1996.

Garcia, Sinikka Gronberg. *Suomi Specialities: Finnish Celebrations, Recipes and Traditions*. Iowa City, IA: Pentfield Press, 1998.

Gianakura, Peter C. *The American Café, Reflections from the Grill*. Sault Ste. Marie, MI: privately published, 2009.

Harrison, Jim. *Returning to Earth*. New York: Grove Press, 2007.

———. *True North*. New York: Grove Press, 2004.

Hemingway, Ernest. "Big Two-Hearted River." In *The Nick Adams Stories*, edited by Philip Young. New York: Bantam, 1973.

Herd, Tim. *Maple Sugar, from Sap to Syrup: The History, Lore and How-To behind This Sweet Treat*. North Adams, MA: Storey Publishing, 2010.

Hobart, Henry. *Copper Country Journal: The Diary of Schoolmaster Henry Hobart, 1863–1864*. Edited by Philip P. Mason. Detroit, MI: Wayne State University Press, 1991.

Kalm, Peter. "The Method for Making Spruce Beer as Practiced in North America, from the Letters of P. Kalm Sent to the Swedish Academy." *Gentleman's Magazine and Historical Chronicle* 22 (September 1752): 399–400.

———. *Travels in North America*. Edited by Adolph B. Benson. New York: Dover Publications, 1987.

Kent, Timothy J. *Ft. Pontchartrain at Detroit: A Guide to the Daily Lives of Fur Trade and Military Personnel, Settlers, and Missionaries at French Posts*. 2 vols. Ossineke, MI: Silver Fox Enterprise, 2001.

Keweenaw Bay Ojibwa Community College Ojibwa Recipe Book. L'Anse, MI: Keweenaw Bay Ojibwa Community College, 2003.

Kisabeth, Dona Lynne. "The Geography of Restaurants: A Case Study in Michigan's Upper Peninsula." Master's thesis, Oklahoma State University, 2000.

Kluck, Kevin R., and Randall J. Kluck. *Yooper Bars: Visit the Finest Bars in the Upper Peninsula.* Hancock, MI: Whiskey River Publishing, 2012.

Kohl, Johann G. *Kitchi-Gami: Life among the Lake Superior Ojibway.* St. Paul: Minnesota Historical Society Press, 1985.

Kosky, William Van. "Marquette County's Fizz Factories." *Michigan History,* January–February 2003, 48–54.

Kowlaski, Jake. "UP Food: A Taste of History." *Marquette Mining Journal,* November 10, 1996.

Ladies Aid Society. *Copper Country Cookery.* Laurium, MI: Ladies Aid Society of the Laurium Methodist Episcopal Church, 1902.

Ladies Aid Society. *The Munising's Tried and True Cookbook, 1930.* Munising, MI: Ladies Aid Society of the First Presbyterian Church, 1930.

Ladies of the Presbyterian Church. *Ishpeming Cookbook.* Marquette, MI: Mining Journal Print, 1896.

Landon, David R. "'Berries in Season': Seeds from the Industrial Town of Fayette, Michigan." *Michigan Archaeologist* 43, no. 1 (March 1997): 26–33.

Lankton, Larry. "'A Lapful of Apples': Foodways of the Far North." In *Beyond the Boundaries: Life and Landscape at the Lake Superior Copper Mines, 1840–1875,* by Larry Lankton. New York: Oxford University Press, 1997.

Legwold, Gary. *The Last Word on Lutefisk: True Tales of Cod and Tradition.* Minneapolis, MN: Conrad Henry Press, 1996.

Liffring-Zug Bourret, Joan, et al., eds. *Finnish Touches: Recipes and Traditions.* Iowa City, IA: Penfield Books, 2002.

Lockwood, William G., and Yvonne R. Lockwood. "Finnish American Milk Products in the Northwoods." In *Milk: Beyond Dairy. Proceedings of the Oxford Symposium on Food and Cookery 1999,* edited by Harlan Walker, 232–39. Totnes, UK: Prospect Books, 2000.

———. "Pasties in Michigan: Foodways, Interethnic Relations and Cultural Dynamics." In *Creative Ethnicity,* edited by Stephen Stern and John Allan Cicala, 3–20. Logan: Utah State University Press, 1991.

———. "Pasties in Michigan's Upper Peninsula Foodways: Interethnic Relations and Regionalism." In *The Taste of American Place,* edited by Barbara G. Shortridge and James R. Shortridge. Lanham, MD: Rowman Littlefield, 1998.

Lockwood, Yvonne R., with Anne Kaplan. "Upper Great Lakes Foodways." In *American Sampler Cookbook,* edited by Katherine and Thomas Kurlin, 172–86. Washington, D.C.: Smithsonian Institution Press, n.d.

Mackinac Fudge Recipes: 16 Delicious Fudge Recipes. Berrien Center, MI: Penrod/Hiawatha, n.d.

Magnaghi, Russell M. "Celebrating the Smelt: The UP Jamborees." *Chronicle* (Historical Society of Michigan) 43, no. 3 (Fall 2020): 26–28.

———. "The Cornish Pasty: Its History and Lore." In *A Sense of Place: Michigan's Upper Peninsula*, edited by Russell M. Magnaghi and Michael T. Marsden, 119–34. Marquette: Northern Michigan University Press, 1997.

———. "Euro-American Commercial Fishing in the Eastern Upper Peninsula." *Rural Insights* (November 2020).

———. "The 'Eyes' Have It: UP Potatoes." *Michigan History* 104, no. 3 (May–June 2020): 46–51.

———. "Foodways of the Upper Peninsula." In *A Sense of Place: Michigan's Upper Peninsula*, edited by Russell M. Magnaghi and Michael T. Marsden, 109–18. Marquette: Northern Michigan University Press, 1997.

———. *Huron, Ottawa and French Settlement at St. Ignace, Michigan, 1670–1751.* St. Ignace, MI: Downtown Development Agency, 1989.

———. "The Mystery of the Cudighi Solved." *Chronicle* 39, no. 4 (Winter 2017): 43.

———. "The Ojibwa in Marquette, Michigan, Pre-History to the Opening of the Mining Frontier." *Upper Country, Journal of the Lake Superior Region* 7 (2019): 40–54.

———. "The Pasty, a Hearty Heritage." *Michigan History* 99, no. 4 (July–August 2015): 36–39.

———. *Prohibition in the Upper Peninsula: Booze & Bootleggers on the Border.* Charleston, SC: The History Press, 2017.

———. *Upper Peninsula Beer: A History of Brewing above the Bridge.* Charleston, SC: The History Press, 2015.

———. "What to Do with Song Birds?" *Michigan Oral History Association Newsletter* (Spring 2021).

Magnaghi, Russell M., and David Smith. *Apple Culture in the Upper Peninsula and Border Wisconsin.* Marquette, MI: 906 Heritage Press, 2019.

Marietti, Justin. "Mangiamo: 'Let's Eat,' Ralph's Italian Deli: A Staple for More than 50 Years." *Marquette Mining Journal*, part C, April 16, 2016.

May, George S. *The Mess at Mackinac or, 'No More Sagamity for Me, Thank You!'* Mackinac Island, MI: Mackinac Island State Park Commission, 1964.

McCabe, John. *Grand Hotel, Mackinac Island.* Sault Ste. Marie, MI: Unicorn Press, 1987.

McGinn, Sterling. "When Newberry Was the Celery City." *Newberry News*, June 10, 2020.

McKenna, Paula K. *Ships of the Great Lakes Cookbook: Discover Their Culinary Legends.* N.p.: Creative Characters Publishing Group, 2001.

Noble, Vergil E., Jr. "In Dire Straits: Subsistence Patterns at Mackinac." *Michigan Archaeologist* 29, no. 3 (September 1983): 29–48.

Ojäkängäs, Beatrice A. *The Finnish Cookbook.* New York: Crown Publishers, Inc., 1964.

Osborn, Chase S. *Northwoods Sketches.* Lansing: Historical Society of Michigan, 1949.

Palmer Firemen's Auxiliary. *Wild Game Recipes.* St. Paul, MN: Gateway Fund Raising Systems, Inc., [circa 1975].

Pascoe, Ann. *Cornish Recipes.* Redruth, Cornwall, UK: Tor Mark Press, 1988, 2006.

Pearce, Deb. *Mise-en-Place: A Wildcat Kitchen.* Marquette: Northern Michigan University Hospitality Tourism Management, [2021].

Pellowe, Susan. *Saffron & Currants: A Cornish Heritage Cookbook.* Aurora, IL: Renard Productions, 1989; rev. ed., 1998.

Phillips, Michael E. *Morel Mushrooms: The Best Kept Secrets Revealed.* Morrisville, NC: Lulu Publishing, 2011.

Porter, Phil. *A Desirable Station: Soldier Life at Fort Mackinac, 1867–1895.* Mackinac Island, MI: Mackinac State Historic Parks, 2003.

———. "The Eagle at Mackinac: The Establishment of United States Military and Civil Authority on Mackinac Island, 1796–1802." *Reports in Mackinac History and Archaeology* 11. Mackinac Island, MI: Mackinac State Historic Parks, 1991.

———. *Fudge: Mackinac's Sweet Souvenir.* Mackinac Island, MI: Mackinac State Historic Parks, 2001.

Reinhardt, Martin, L. Lancaster and April Lindala. *Decolonization Diet Project Cookbook.* Marquette: Northern Michigan University, Center for Native American Studies, 2016.

Savage, Kay. "From the Mines to the Supermarket: The Pasty Debate Lives On." *Chronicle* (Historical Society of Michigan) 16, no. 1 (Spring 1980): 12–15.

Schladorn, Mary Naasko, ed. *Kangas Family Centennial Cookbook, 1888–1988.* Audubon, IA: Jumbo Jack's Cookbook Co., 1988.

Scott, Elizabeth M. *French Subsistence at Michilimackinac, 1715–1781: The Clergy and the Traders.* Archaeological Completion Report Series, no. 9. Mackinac Island, MI: Mackinac Island State Park Commission, 1985.

———. "'Such Diet as Benefitted His Station as Clerk': The Archaeology of Subsistence and Cultural Diversity at Fort Michilimackinac, 1761–1781." PhD dissertation, University of Minnesota, 1991.

Swedish Recipes Old and New. Chicago: American Daughters of Sweden, 1953.

Thwaites, Reuben G., ed. *The Jesuit Relations and Allied Documents.* 73 vols. New York: Pageant Book Co., 1959.

Traver, Robert. *Danny and the Boys, Being Some Legends of Hungry Hollow.* 1951; repr., Detroit, MI: Wayne State University Press, 1987.

Treacy, Ann O'Brien. "Pasties, Our Regional Comfort Food." *Lake Superior Magazine,* January 1, 2007, 1–6.

Valli, Mina. *Keittokirjä/Cookbook.* 3rd ed. Superior, WI: Tyomies Society, 1923.

Vennum, Thomas, Jr. *Wild Rice and the Ojibway People.* St. Paul: Minnesota Historical Society Press, 2004.

Warner, Edward S. "Victuals and Cooks in the American Great Lakes Commercial Trade under Sail." *Inland Seas* 61, no. 2 (Summer 2005): 125–30.

Whitman, Yvonne. "Unshakable Devotion Keeps Brownstone Inn Thriving for More than 70 Years." *Michigan Country Lines* 36, no. 10 (November–December 2016): 12–13.

Widder, Keith R. *Reveille till Taps: Soldier Life at Fort Mackinac, 1780–1895.* Mackinac Island, MI: Mackinac State Historic Parks, 1972.

Index

INDEX

About the Author

Russell M. Magnaghi, noted and award-winning historian of Michigan's Upper Peninsula, has had a four-decades-long interest in and curiosity about the food and beverage of the region. However, his origins go back to San Francisco, California, where his family operated the Swiss Italian Sausage Factory, raised fruit trees in Santa Clara (now Silicon Valley) and made home-brew and dago red. In the Upper Peninsula, he has pursued the study of food and beverage and interviewed many old-timers who shared their fascinating stories. He and his wife frequently enjoy dining at the Grand Hotel on Mackinac Island or a whitefish dinner at home overlooking Lake Superior. He is the author of numerous food-related articles on the UP, along with a number of books, the most recent being *Upper Peninsula Beer: A History of Brewing across the Bridge* and *Prohibition in the Upper Peninsula: Booze and Bootleggers on the Border*. A graduate of the University of San Francisco and St. Louis University, he taught for forty-five years at Northern Michigan University. He and his wife, Diane, reside in Marquette, Michigan.

Visit us at
www.historypress.com